# A GOD OF MIRACLES

*A God of Miracles*
- healing from God's Word
*the story about Charles Ndifon*
*By Henri Nissen*

© *Copyright 2003*
*Scandinavia Publishing House*
*Drejervej 15,3*
*DK-2400 Copenhagen NV*
*Tlf. +45 35 31 03 30*
*www.scanpublishing.dk*

*Cover: Grafix/Benny Alex*
*Layout: Henri Nissen*
*Print: Poland*
*ISBN 87 7247 0178*

# Contents:

*I would like to thank Jan Due-Christensen and René Ottesen, ministers in Odense and Copenhagen, and journalists Bodil Harild, Copenhagen and Bornholm, Svend Løbner Madsen, Vejen, Louise Ø. Poulsen, Odense, Orla Fredensborg Møller, Århus, Ginny McInnes, Sooky News Mirror, Lauren Hopkins from Scarborough Evening News for transcripts, photos and help in supplying information for this book. My thanks also to Birthe, Henrik, Maj-Britt and John Nissen for proofreading, help with Bible references and moral support.*

*Thanks also to Angel Production, TV2 and TV2 Funen for permission to use TV images from their programs. A special thanks to Donna and Charles Ndifon for permission to use material and their cooperation to make this book possible.*

# Part 1

# Miracles
# abound

# Supernatural Powers

**The lame walk, the blind see, the deaf hear...**
**Is there a God after all?**
**Danes had virtually given up on church and Christianity,**
**when suddenly something happened that abruptly**
**changed the prejudices of many...**

## It all began with a fairly spooky evening

TV producer, Thomas Breinholt, was visiting Michael Rex, who is an editor for TV2. He had told him that 'weird' things happened at his house. Suddenly, while they were sitting in his lounge room, they heard a strange sound coming from the hall. In that instant, a picture fell off the wall and literally floated three meters and landed on the floor. Later there was a noise as if the front door had opened. But when they looked it was still shut. This happened several times...

Neither Breinholt nor Rex knew how to explain these strange "hauntings". But since Breinholt was in the middle of making a featurefilm about spiritist, Frank Munkø, he wanted to see whether the spiritist could banish the ghosts.

"I actually expected it to be a bit comical. I thought we were going to see a man run around chanting, talking to the spirits", he said later in an interview.[1]

"At that time I had no idea what these recordings would lead to, but they have since been shown, unedited, in the TV series "Supernatural Powers", in which Michael's flat was 'cleansed of a ghost', and his glass table exploded!"

## "Supernatural Powers"

"The day after the recordings in Michael's flat, I was still very shocked about what we had witnessed. I got to work on the "editing", and looked through the tape, frame by frame, to see if I could find a natural explanation for what had happened. But I couldn't! I was quite puzzled and couldn't understand it. Since I had a lot of other projects underway at the same time, I decided to put the segment on the shelf. But some colleagues from *TV2 Lorry* (a government owned regional TV channel in Copenhagen) heard what had happened, and they were virtually climbing over each other to see the tapes.

It became apparent that we had succeeded in making some 'spiritual TV' which affected people. It may perhaps have been a completely new way to use the media – to make television about the occult and the supernatural world. Normally this would be an impossible task, because you can't see the spiritual; but in this case you could see the people's reactions.

At the same time, I realized that numerous people have had spiritual experiences, but it was just something that people don't talk about. The idea therefore slowly took shape for me, to make a series. That series became 'Supernatural Powers'".

*TV-producer Thomas Breinholt*

## A mixed bag

As we will see later, Danes are probably one of the most irreligious peoples in the world. The idea of a spiritual reality has been beaten down, time and again – even by the church which has preached an intellectual, common-sense Christianity with no feelings or fellowship, and hardly any spiritual dimension. Astonishingly little has been preached about the Holy Spirit and the supernatural in the old Danish Medieval churches, despite the fact that the beautiful old murals depict both demons and angels.

Therefore, the TV series "Supernatural Powers", along with some other events, became a real eye-opener. They didn't just shake the TV producer's worldview, they also shook that of most of the viewers.

The Supernatural Powers series wasn't a Christian series. It was a mixed bag. They presented programs on many different spiritual phenomena. But one of the programs had a special impact on the audience. After that program, the producer received over one thousand letters. That was the program on the healing preacher, Charles Ndifon:

"I remember I was sitting watching the TV2 news where there was an item about Charles Ndifon", explains TV producer, Thomas Breinholt. "It was one of those clips where you see something 'churchy', and some people singing to some strange music. If it was going to work, we would have to get hold of someone who didn't believe in Jesus and who had a documented illness – and follow him up for a long time. We called Roger Pedersen, who after some consideration, came along to Ringkøbing where the meetings with Ndifon were held.

## Roger was the viewers' representative

"When we got to Ringkøbing we were met by that "American hallelujah" tone, and that has always been like a red rag to me. Our expectations were therefore palpably apparent. But we also had Roger, who was just as reserved, and he was the viewers' representative – he was the one whom everyone could identify with.

At the same time, Charles Ndifon was an inspired communicator. And as the evening raced on we became more and more dumbfounded. I went around and talked to several people. There was someone there on crutches. He was quickly dragged forward – and threw away his crutches.

I almost choked on my vanilla cake, but I was also skeptical, so my next thought was: 'He's been planted! They might have taken him along to pep up the meeting'. That's the way I have been raised to think. My scientific background involves questioning everything I see", says Thomas Breinholt. Thomas was originally trained as an agronomist at the Danish Royal Veterinary and Agricultural University, and only ended up working with the television media by chance.

## Roger's miracle – fantastic...

"Then it was Roger's turn. He laid his hand on the bad eye – and the miracle happened! I was so moved when I stood in front of Roger and saw that he could see again. The whole team stood with tears in our eyes, it was simply impossible to maintain professional distance when something like that happened. It was fantastic.

The next day I tried to get my feet back on the ground again. Was it something psychological? Was it something Roger had generated himself? My mind was full of questions. But I couldn't explain away the fact that Roger had been healed. This was also confirmed for us by the hospital later.

The program from Ringkøbing is still one of my favorite programs. Before our very eyes, we see a person experience a powerful, positive, life transformation.

## The ministers were disappointing

When were making "Supernatural Powers", I tried to get some ministers from the national church to appear on the program. But none wanted to be involved. Even ministers from the free (non-state) churches were hard to get hold of. Christians have been very reluctant to come out of their hiding holes – usually with an excuse about needing to be careful of the "victims". But even when the "victims" have wanted to tell their stories, the ministers have still not wanted to be involved.

I was also surprised that most national church ministers don't place any spiritual content in the Bible. I think the subject is surrounded by far too much taboo. It is quite simply disappointing that Christians won't broach a

*Roger Pedersen and Charles Ndifon meet for the first time, after Roger's eyes were healed during the meeting. The healing resounded throughout the whole country, as it turned out that TV2 had brought Roger along as a "guinea pig". Ndifon actually didn't notice Roger until after the miracle had happened.*

*Charles Ndifon, speaking for the first time in Denmark. This took place in the tiny "Jesus church" in Ringkøbing, which was started by a group of youths and meets in a local sports centre in the town.*

subject which interests so many people.

Ministers and the church need to come onto the field and give their version of this. Otherwise it will all be left to the New Age market, which is a cowboy land made up of half-disguised charlatans mixed with people who have genuine intentions. But this market doesn't have any form of quality control," says Thomas Breinholt.

## A spiritual journey of discovery

For Thomas Breinholt, the series also had such personal significance that he had to start investigating how things actually can be explained:

"'Supernatual Powers' has been like a journey for me. I thought the world looked a certain way. But my work with the program gave me some huge challenges in getting things to fit together. I had to therefore investigate various models of explanation which lie outside our rational world of explanation. So I started reading about Buddha, Islam, Christian mysticism and spiritism.

This journey has convinced me that there are dimensions to our existence which lie outside our three-dimensional comprehension.

My personal experience has been that Christian theology has had the greatest significance to me. This is what I am interested in. No doubt this is linked to the fact that I have grown up in a Christian country. But what the ultimate truth is, I don't know. I think I will only discover it when I stand before the gates of heaven", Thomas Breinholt concludes.

## Your own spiritual journey?

This book is also a "spiritual journey" - or a guide - into a spiritual world which the greater part of science and our schoolbooks throughout the entire 20th century have denied exists. How should the man on the street handle these powers, without being knocked off his feet?

This books is first and foremost about Charles Ndifon – the Nigerian who changed the Danes' view of the spiritual, and who is now becoming more and more active throughout the whole world.

In the chapters which follow we will look more closely at who Charles Ndifon actually is; what the worldview he works in is based on; and what possible reason there might be for why so much happens when he prays for the sick.

We will hear his explanation for why the normal physical laws can apparently be broken, and people can be healed – just as in the time of Jesus.

We will meet some of the many people who have now personally experienced healing in their own bodies.

We will also look more closely at why some are not healed, why some are first healed after some time, and why some apparently "lose" their healing again. We will take a look at a statistical/medical study of some of the Danes who were "healed".

We will look at some of the sensational scientific studies which show that prayer actually has an effect.

Enjoy your journey!

Note 1: Interview with René Ottesen, KKR/TV, presented in the KE magazine, December 2001, quoted by permission.

# Commotion in Ringkøbing

**The story actually begins even earlier.**
**Before February 2000.**

The story begins far out in windswept Ringkøbing, beside the North Sea, where a small group of youths have formed their own "Jesus Church" in an uprising against the boring official state church.

There are truly only about fifteen youths, and their just as young "minister", Peter Skov, has to work in the discount store, Netto, to support himself. But he is newly wed, to Mona, and full of optimism, and they are convinced that Christianity is much more than what most people think it is:

So Peter searched on the Internet for people and places in the world where something was happening. He wanted to find something on miracles – and not just in the third world, but in the West. He kept running into the same name: Charles Ndifon. Originally, Charles comes from Nigeria in Africa, but he now lives in Rhode Island in the USA.

"I thought it sounded incredibly exciting, so I got hold of some tapes from a church in Canada where he had been. The tapes convinced me that it was a man like Ndifon we needed in Denmark, if there was really going to be a spiritual breakthrough", says Peter Skov.

*"What did you do?"*

"I simply called

*Two young people, Mona and Peter Skov, invited Ndifon to Denmark*

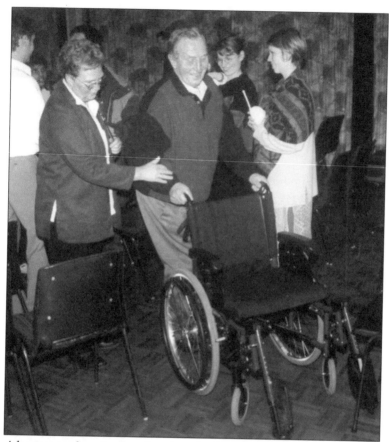

*A happy man has stood up from his wheelchair and is testing out his legs during these dramatic days in Ringkøbing. He was allegedly healed of diabetes and pain in his legs.*

him and asked if he would come to Denmark."

*"What did he say?"*

"He was very positive about the idea. He said that we should expect miracles and wonders to happen."

*"What did it cost?"*

"It was going to end up costing about two thousand five hundred pounds all up, for travel for him and his colleagues, hire of a venue, advertising, hotel accommodation, etc. (They actually stayed at a youth hostel – but we have a very nice youth hostel here in Ringkøbing!)"

"How did such a small group of youths dare to venture out into something like this?"

"We had saved up about two thousand five hundred pounds because we hadn't employed anyone yet, and we hadn't bought our own building - we just rented our way into the local ROFI sports center. So we decided to use this money on the meetings."

## Teaching on healing

Peter and company then arranged a series of meetings in February 2000.

Charles Ndifon came and ran meetings both morning and evening in the ROFI center, from Wednesday the 9th to Sunday 13 February 2000. In the mornings there was teaching on biblical healings and how these miracles can also happen today through the individual Christian. The youths in the church were taught how they should pray for the healing of the sick – and many continue to do so. Now there are healing meetings which are held on the last Thursday of each month in the Jesus church – in a room in the ROFI.

Even though the morning meetings were intended for internal training, there were always some people that turned up who wanted to be healed, so Charles Ndifon generally ended up praying for sick people anyway.

Orla Fredensborg Møller was at one of the morning meetings and recalls:

"After Charles Ndifon had spoken for one and a half hours, he paused and said that he would pray for those who needed prayer, before he got on to what he actually had planned to say.

A lady with Alzheimer's disease apparently gained some relief; a man experienced that the pain in his legs disappeared; two people with asthma were healed, etc. The meeting continued two and a half hours past the planned close, but Charles couldn't tear himself away from praying for people, and speaking on the theme: living each day in victorious faith.

## Free entry

In the evening there were proper healing meetings, where entry was, of course, free. That was a surprise for the non-churchgoing Danes who came to be healed. But in churches one doesn't normally charge an entry fee, rather one encourages the participants to give voluntarily as they are able to cover the expenses.

As each day passed, more and more people came to the meetings, and the miraculous healings increased each evening.

"Of course we believed and hoped that something big would happen, but we hadn't even dreamt that so much would happen", says Peter, and adds, "Or of the things which have happened since…"

*"Why did your meetings become so widely known?"*

"Many believe it was because of the TV series "Supernatural Powers", but that program was only broadcast six months later – in the autumn. But there was a small feature in the nationwide TV2 News on Wednesday evening, and in the nationwide DR1 TV channel's very popular program, *19-Direkte*. That created enormous interest. People could see that something was really happening. The telephone was almost glowing. People from all over the country called

*"God's Word is His medicine", Ndifon proclaims, "Fear the Lord and shun evil; this will bring health to your body…' he quotes from Proverbs 3:8.*

and asked where it was happening and how they could come into contact with Charles Ndifon. We had expected that we could perhaps ferret out sixty to seventy people from the churches in Ringkøbing. But on Saturday evening alone, three hundred and fifty people came, and they weren't locals.

We were not at all prepared for all the people who flocked to us from all over the country, with the most terrible illnesses", says Peter.

## Can I speak to the healer?

"People always asked for *the healer*", says Mona Skov.

"They had trouble understanding that it is God who heals, and not the healer. Someone asked me: 'Can he heal at a distance?' We found that many people were willing to travel from far away, and also to pay to come in and be prayed for – they were surprised that the meetings were free."

A lady told Mona on the phone about the guru, Sai-Baba from India, whom she believed also healed people by God's power. In the end Mona had to give up trying to explain that it wasn't actually the same God on view.

(That was before *TV-avisen*, a news program, exposed Sai-Baba as a conjurer and a pedophile in a number of features in February 2002).

Peter adds, "People today have never heard of a healing evangelist, and rarely know how a Christian healing meeting is run. The concepts and forms people are used to come from the New Age environment and alternative forms of treatment."

At most of the evening meetings there were people present who had received alternative treatments and who thought it had to be the same power at work here. But they were amazed that so much time was spent on teaching from the Bible…

## No magic ability?

They found out that Charles Ndifon didn't claim to have any special healing power or magic ability himself, as some had imagined.

He simply preached Christianity. But not the form of Christianity which most people associated with the state church. Charles Ndifon took it quite literally when Jesus healed and said that his followers should do the same.

The difference between Ndifon's Christianity and "normal" Christianity was apparently that he believed it without reservation – and therefore it worked…

His message in Ringkøbing was that a simple word said in faith can save and heal people.

## "God's word is His medicine"

Orla F.Møller reports from one of the first meetings with Ndifon, in the Christian weekly magazine, Udfordringen (the Challenge):

"He pulled out some examples from the New Testament: Mary showed faith when she was told that she would be the mother of the Savior: 'May it be to me as you have said' (Luke 1:38). And the Roman officer whose servant was sick and about to die, expressed it like this: 'But say the word, and my servant will be healed' (Luke 7:7).

Charles Ndifon's point is that we should take God's word at face value when He says, ' I am the LORD , who heals you!' (Exodus 15:26); and when the scriptures clearly say: 'Surely he took up our infirmities and carried our sorrows.' (Isaiah 53:4). 'God's Word is His medicine', Ndifon proclaims as he splashes Bible quotes about, 'Fear the Lord and shun evil; this will bring health to your body…' (Proverbs 3:8).

He continues: 'Many people expect that if they are going to be healed by God's power, it has to be immediate. But sometimes healing happens slowly.

If your doctor gives you medicine and it doesn't work the first day, do you throw it out? No, you follow the instructions on the prescription and continue until there is a result. Follow the instructions in God's Word and you will be healed! As you speak God's Word in faith, your healing begins – if you doubt, you stop the process.'

## Traditional churches obstruct healing

Charles Ndifon speaks on one of the main reasons that many are not healed:

"Traditional churches have taught for years that you shouldn't expect God to intervene with miracles like he did in the time of the apostles. I have to laugh when I think about the fact that the religious leaders in Jesus' time also thought the same way. They were offended when he healed people. But Jesus rebuked them and said:

"...*You have set aside the commands of God in order to observe your own traditions*".

I grew up in a traditional religious home myself, where I went to church and lived as I was meant to, but my faith was dead. People feel secure in traditions and don't dare to leap out in faith in God. That's why I teach for a long time before I begin to pray for people; I want to awaken and strengthen their faith, because "faith comes from hearing the message".

As Christians we don't doubt for a moment that God wants all to be saved, but we do doubt whether he wants all to be healed. God doesn't just want your soul to become whole, but your body as well. Many people have listened to incorrect teaching for tventy to thirty years, and we have to fix up a lot of things in just five days here, before they can receive their miracle!"

## Reach out for Jesus – not me!

On Sunday Charles Ndifon was the guest preacher in the Pentecostal church in Holstebro. Peter Skov started by witnessing to the healings of the last few days.

In his opinion, the most noteworthy ones took place when Charles Ndifon, after an interview on Ringkøbing Local Radio had spontaneously prayed for several of the studio hosts and members of the production team, who had also been healed!

*This man with back problems couldn't walk without pain. He was healed as he stood in the meeting in Rinkøbing. It seemed as if God pulled his spine into place!*

After some teaching, Ndifon showed again how easy it is to be healed by God's power.

"It is very easy to get healed – the difficult thing is to trust in God and believe that Jesus has borne your illness."

People were also greatly surprised that he wouldn't lay hands on each person. But Ndifon explained, "In the Bible it says that everyone who touched Jesus was healed (Matthew 14:36). The reason I don't touch you is to leave room for you to reach out for Jesus! We so often say, 'God, touch me! But now I want you to show that you believe that it isn't me but God who heals you."

Ndifon also prayed for a woman with one short leg, and said, "Can you see it's growing? It will become just as long as the other one. "

When the woman left the church just after noon she was still limping, but she smiled, "It's just because one of my shoes is too high now!"

## Miracle days in Ringkøbing

During the hectic days with Ndifon, Peter Skov sent out an excited email, in which he breathlessly, in point form, talked about everything that was happening around him:

"Woman with a hip problem, where one leg was longer than the other. The short leg grew out!"

"Man, hearing impaired in both ears, mainly the left. Hearing aid taken out, and he could hear perfectly!"

"An old man, very poor hearing in both ears. Totally healed – can hear from several meters away. Also had arthritis in knee and hip. Got much better, the pain disappeared!"

"Woman with a bad shoulder. Got much better!"

"Young man with breathing problems. Can breathe without any difficulty (after a run)!"

"Woman with pain in one knee, one leg longer than the other. Pain gone, and the leg grew out to the same length!"

"Man with back problems, couldn't walk without pain. Healed as he stood in the meeting. Seemed as if God pulled his spine into place!"

"Woman with a crooked back (10cm difference in shoulder height), legs different lengths and pain in her back after an accident. Her shoulder came up to the same level, her legs became the same length, and she moved her body from side to side – she hadn't been able to do that for 8 years!

"Man with pinched nerves after a disk operation, which gives heart problems, neck and back pain. The pain disappeared more and more!"

"Woman with arthritic back pain. Totally healed, no pain!"

"Young man with two bad knees due to football and bad

twisting in his knee. His knee still clicks, but the pain is completely gone!"

"Woman with a crooked back and leg pain for 3 years due to pinched nerve. Pain gone and can touch the ground with her fingertips!"

"Man with neck pain for forty two years after whiplash. Pain completely gone!"

"Woman with lung cancer causing pain. The doctors had given up doing anything. The pain disappeared completely (Waiting now for Doctor confirmation)!"

"Man with back and neck problems. Totally healed!"

In addition to this, at this afternoon's meeting (Thursday), a young man was healed of pain and reduced hearing in his left ear. He had had it for years, and immediately felt that the pain was gone! There were also others with back pain and several other afflictions who were healed!

This evening I will just briefly mention that people received healing from reduced mobility in a broken arm and shoulder, one person with sclerosis could move more and more freely the more she exercised her faith and was encouraged to action.

A person with brain damage due to a heart attack could immediately feel they had been totally healed after prayer, etc., etc.

COME YOURSELF AND EXPERIENCE IT – IT'S NOW IT'S HAPPENING – IN THESE DAYS, FOR THESE DAYS ARE MIRACLE DAYS!

**Secret guest:** *Roger Pedersen from Copenhagen was TV2's secret guest and became the key figure in TV2 Zulu's feature. Ndifon actually didn't notice Roger until later, after the miracle had happened. Roger had simply "received Jesus", when Charles Ndifon encouraged everyone to do so. And suddenly he could see normally...*

# Roger's story

## TV-2 visits with a secret guest

Saturday evening so many people came to Ringkøbing that they had to push the stage back and cram more chairs into the room. But it didn't help much, the room was still overflowing at the evening meeting.

The first forty five minutes passed with Christian youth songs of praise, an introduction, and a voluntary collection for *Christ Love Ministries*, which is Charles Ndifon's office and organization.

Then Charles Ndifon finally came in – pursued closely by a TV-team.

It was Thomas Breinholt and his team, who were making a program for "Supernatural Powers". Neither Ndifon nor anyone else had any idea that they had also brought along a secret test person, who was already sitting in the hall. A very skeptical Roger Pedersen, who didn't have any big expectations. The idea was to use him as a guinea pig. Afterwards they would check if anything had happened. And if not, they could prove to the whole world that it was deception.

### Young man threw away his crutches

That evening, Charles broke with his custom of a long introductory talk, and fairly quickly called people forward with pain in their legs and other specific afflictions which he apparently knew about, without knowing the person beforehand.

It wasn't long either before a young man who hadn't been able to stand without crutches for three years, in front of the cameras, handed over his crutches to Ndifon and ran and jumped down the aisle rejoicing. (See the later chapter with Kristian Primdahl "Healed in front of the cameras")

Charles returned to his teaching, "This evening you have to stop limiting God. You saw the man with the crutches: he believed, he was happy and he was set free. Those of you who are here with pain and illness, I don't know you, but God knows you and loves you. His power is here today to heal you. The Jesus who is described in the Bible is here tonight with the same power

23

as he had then. I don't need to touch you for you to be healed. God's power is present and can heal you where you sit!"

An elderly lady came who was blind due to diabetes.

Ndifon asked her, "Do you believe that Jesus took your illness upon himself when he died? If Jesus took your illness, do you need to be blind or have diabetes?"

She answered boldly "No".

"OK, then take off your dark glasses and let's check your vision. How many fingers am I holding up in front of you?" And to her own and the whole hall's amazement, she answered correctly – she could see! It was so simple and so unpretentious.

## Expect a miracle!

About 60 people came forward when Charles asked the gathering who would like to receive Jesus. Just prior to this he had explained, based on Hebrews chapter 9 and elsewhere, that Jesus bore everyone's guilt when he died. "Many want healing but not the Healer", he preached. "In order to be healed, Jesus has to live in you; because when he lives in you, his power will drive out all illness! Is that good news for you?"

While New Testaments were being handed out to the recent converts by the members of the Jesus church, Charles began to explain that he wouldn't lay hands on everyone, but that he would pray a prayer while everyone who was sick laid hands on themselves.

"When I pray, be happy and believe. After the prayer, check your pain and do something you have never been able to do before." There was some confusion, as most people wanted to go to the front and be prayed for, but Charles managed to get everyone quiet, and explained the procedure again and again, "When you feel an improvement, say: Thank you Jesus; and keep acting on your faith. If you just sit and look at the others you will block your healing. You shouldn't hope you will be healed – expect it!"

Many rejoiced loudly about the fact that the pain in their bodies had disappeared, while Charles went around and helped people, and prayed for them again where necessary.

A man with paralysis and diabetes got up from his wheelchair and pushed it happily out of the hall.

The TV team were busy running around talking with the many people who had experienced a miracle. The correspondent from *Udfordringen* magazine, Orla Møller, overheard the TV people say to each other, "This is absolutely crazy! We have just filmed a guy who hasn't been able to run for ten years, and now he's dashing around the courtyard!"

## The secret person

The man who had come with the TV team had a patch over one eye.

Roger had had an accident in which he had suffered a skull fracture. As a result one eye had lowered, and he had developed chronic vision impairment – so-called double vision.

Charles didn't notice him at all, but he had sat at the back of the hall and had followed the preaching skeptically. At one point, when Charles called upon people to raise their hand and indicate if they wanted to believe in Jesus, he hesitantly raised his hand. Then Charles called upon everyone who had some defect or other, to lay their own hand on the sick place, and he would pray for them. When he was finished, Roger took the patch away from his eye – and "couldn't believe his eyes": He could see completely normally – clearly and distinctly!

The TV team didn't even notice, but found him outside the meeting hall – ecstatic with joy. When he had gathered himself, he went in to Charles Ndifon to thank him.

"But he said I shouldn't thank *him* – but rather go out and tell others about it. And I have been doing that ever since. Not a day goes by, where I don't tell someone what has happened", says Roger Pedersen.[1]

## Drawn curtains

For the previous three months, Roger Pedersen had actually shut himself in behind drawn curtains, deeply depressed about his situation. He was fortunate that one of the technicians at TV2 Zulu knew him, and that the camera team decided to take him along as a "guinea pig", to see if Charles Ndifon could heal.

After the miraculous healing in Ringkøbing, Thomas Breinholt and the team behind "Supernatural Powers" followed up Roger Pedersen. He was examined at the hospital, where they had to concede that something had happened. Naturally the doctor couldn't say whether it was God that had done it, but had to just concede that his eyes were now healed. When asked directly to explain it, he tried to explain the miraculous event with "powerful psychological forces".

## Six months later

Over six months later, on the 7th December, Roger Pedersen was on the TV2 news and confirmed the miracle that had happened – and the host commented, "There is a spiritual revival happening in Denmark."

When Michael Rothstein, a researcher on religion, then tried to explain away Roger's miracle, Roger simply answered, "I just know that I was healed that evening, and that it must have been Jesus that did it."

When asked if he now went to church, he answered with his usual honesty: "No, I think they're too boring…"

On one occasion when he sought advice in a Catholic church in Copenhagen, the priest turned him away, commenting that he didn't believe in miracles. Later Roger sought out some other churches where people believed in healings.

"When I look at the footage today, I can clearly remember what it was like when I came out of the prayer meeting. I went out and tried to read all the signs, and I found that I actually could read them. I almost couldn't believe

*(Angel Production)*

*BEFORE: Roger Pedersen in TV2 Zulu's programme, with a patch over one eye because of his so-called "double vision" which had made life unbearable for him…*

that it had happened. It was incredible", Roger Pedersen told journalist Svend Løbner from Udfordringen, at an interview one year later.[2]

## "It was more powerful"

And if anyone had assumed that it was just TV making a sensation out of nothing , Roger could confirm the opposite:

"It was actually much more powerful than you can see in the program", he explains as he sits outside his cabin on his allotment one cool Sunday morning. A neighbor opens his window and looks at us curiously.

"My neighbors don't think the program was anything special compared to the sight that met them when I came home. I was out of control!

"Everyone has followed this story closely. Those who had seen me while I had bad vision were very surprised, because it is so clear that I have been healed. One of my friends who teaches at a polytechnic, has begun to talk about my experience in his teaching.

*"What has it meant for your faith?"*

*(Angel Production)*

*AFTER: Roger Pedersen after the healing – at home in his flat a couple of months later, being interviewed by TV2 Zulu.*

*"Yes, it was a miracle. I can't see any other explanation. Even if it was a spontaneous healing, why should it happen right at that time – and over just five minutes?"*

"I believe in God, that's for sure, even though I almost still have trouble saying it. And I know he is looking after me. But I have to admit I have trouble giving myself completely.

*"What has this miracle otherwise meant for you?"*

"First and foremost it has meant that I can go to work again, otherwise I would still be on sick leave. But I have also thought a lot about what has happened, and I am not even close to being finished thinking about it yet."

## Prays while watering the flowers

*"Will you start going to a church?"*

"I know that there are churches in Copenhagen which are like the Jesus church, but I don't think I completely fit in. They are nice people and they experience faith in their way, by singing and reading from the Bible together.

But I'm not that fussed about singing, and I think, overall, that way is not my style.

"My faith is more personal. I pray to God as I walk around and water the flowers in the summer, and thank him that they are so beautiful."

*"Have you tried any of the free churches?"*

"Yes, once. I once knew a nurse who invited me along to her church. It was some or other worldwide organization I think.

*"What did you think of it?"*

"They were all very nice, but I guess I'm more inclined towards something where you actually do something or other."

## The church should *do* something

"For example, the church ought to cry out when the Prime Minister, for example, in his New Year speech says that people should come before money. Here in my area the average life expectancy for men is 57 years – the lowest in Europe. But the government is doing nothing."

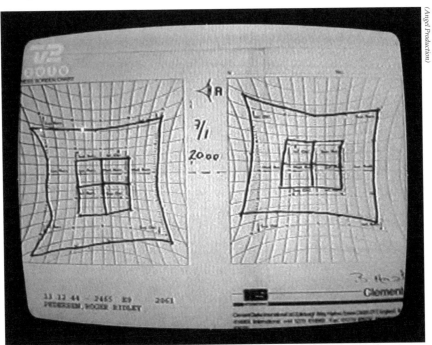

*The programme confirmed, based on examinations at the Danish national hospital, that a change had taken place in Roger Pedersen's vision.*

*"Could the church help?"*

"Absolutely. Take, for example, home care out here. Our neighborhood council has just cut back on home care. At around the same time they used over twenty five thousand pounds on a farewell dinner. That is one and a half home care staff for a whole year!"

"The church could use some of its millions to employ home care staff", Roger suggests. He otherwise only uses churches for quiet meditation.

"I normally go into the Church of Our Lady in the afternoon and stand in front of the large Jesus figure. There isn't usually anyone else there. Then I stand there and talk with Jesus for a while."

## May not be my turn again

Roger Pedersen is amazingly open, given the number of approaches he receives from magazines asking for interviews, from churches wanting him to give a talk, and from people who stop him in the street.

"They congratulate me and want to know a bit more about what happened."

*"Would you let someone pray for you if you happened to suffer from some illness or other?"*

"Possibly. I am sure anyway that I would recommend others to try it. But I would probably think that it wasn't my turn to experience a miracle again. There are so many others that need help. For me, it was a very important experience; it opened my eyes. I might be nervous about trying to repeat it; it is too meaningful for that.

*"Are you still sure that it was a miracle?"*

"Yes, I can't see any other explanation. Even if it was a spontaneous healing, why should it happen right at that time – and over just five minutes?

"I can't see any other explanation."

Note 1 Interview in Udfordringen, week 5, 1 February 2001, page 3.
Note 2 Udfordringen week 5, 1 February 2001, pages 1, 3 and 16.
Photos from the TV program used with the kind permission of Angel Production.

# Healed in front of the cameras

**TV2 filmed Kristian Primdahl, as he threw away his crutches...**

Kristian Primdahl has been crippled for the last ten years due to a knee injury. Despite several stays in hospital and two knee operations, it has only gotten worse. During the three months before the meeting he had walked using crutches to reduce the pain...

It all began at a skating rink in Århus, Denmark's second largest city, where the happy Greenlander really let himself go.

## Destroyed his cruciate ligament on the ice

"One day I had been skating at the skating rink in Århus for one hour and fifty minutes", Kristian recalls.[1]

"I thought about stopping, but since there were only 10 minutes left, I stayed on the ice – and after five minutes I fell."

An ominous pain shot through his leg, and Kristian had to crawl off the ice on all fours. He could hardly walk home.

"It took me forty five minutes to get undressed", he recalls.

When he still couldn't walk after four days, he went to the doctor, who said it was no doubt just a sprain. If it wasn't gone after two days, he should come again – and he did.

"Since I lived in Grenå at that time, I was sent to the hospital there, and from there to the Sports Clinic at Århus County Hospital, where they discovered that I had destroyed my cruciate ligament."

## Constant pain and degenerative arthritis

Initially, Kristian's front cruciate ligament was operated on.

"But my knee was still no good", he explains. "Three more years passed before they operated on my back cruciate ligament."

"Things went better after that, but it still wasn't perfect. The pain came back at regular intervals. After a few years I had constant pain in my knee...

31

Charles Ndifon:
- *Did you expect a miracle when you came here?*
Kristian Primdahl:
- *I always do.*

„If Jesus bore your pain, what would your leg be like now?"
- (Healed!)

„Praise God.... Give me your crutches and walk. Come on, let's take a walk. Move your legs."

*Angel Production*

32

"In February 2000 I had an examination and was given the diagnosis, 'degenerative arthritis'. I was going to be operated on again once I had had a scan done at Skejby hospital.

"But one day in September 2000, one of my friends called me to ask if I could drive her and my brother and sister-in-law to Ringkøbing.

They wanted to go to the healing meeting with an at that time unknown Nigerian evangelist.

## Simply threw away the crutches

Even though Kristian believed that God no doubt *could* heal him, he didn't have the slightest idea that it would happen right in front of the TV2-Zulu camera – the provocative youth channel where the series was first shown.

"I hope I will be completely healed so that I can walk normally again", he said to the TV host, Thomas Breinholt, just before the meeting in Ringkøbing.

Charles Ndifon says that he regularly receives so-called "words of knowledge" from God about people who are suffering certain afflictions. When he stands in front of an unknown crowd, he suddenly says, as he said that evening in Ringkøbing:

"There is someone here who has great pain in their leg."

Kristian Primdahl knew it must be him, so he hobbled up to the platform.

"Why do you walk on crutches?", Ndifon asked.

"I can't walk without them", answered Kristian. "Otherwise the pain is simply too great."

"If Jesus bore your pain, what would your leg be like now?" continued Ndifon.

"Healed", answered Kristian spontaneously.

"Well, throw away your crutches and move your legs", answered Charles Ndifon. "Come on, let's take a walk."

"I was honestly quite surprised when Charles asked me for the crutches, and it took me a while to pull myself together and put weight on my leg."

"I had trouble believing that a short prayer could sort out what the doctors had not been able to do. But there was nothing resembling pain in my knee any more."

"A powerful heat spread throughout my body. After he had prayed for me, the heat rushed down into my right knee, where it gathered."

Kristian let go of his crutches and walked easily across the carpet, and then shouted: "Thank you Jesus!"

## The healing has lasted

Later TV2-Zulu's camera caught up with Kristian again out in the foyer, where the happy Greenlander was running back and forth, in euphoria:

"My whole body became hot, and whoosh, a stream went down into my knee. And then the pain was gone", he explained in the program.

*Kristian has exchanged his crutches for roller skates*

Some months later, TV2-Zulu filmed him again – skating around on roller skates. This happened as part of a follow-up program where they checked up on whether the healings had lasted. As recently as March 2002 I asked him again:

*"How are things going now?"*

"Since my healing, I haven't had any pain in my knee – except if I have twisted my leg. I have had much more energy left over since the healing."

*"What has the healing meant for your spiritual life?"*

"My immediate response is that it is the same as before. The difference is, though, that I now know I can pray for anything – and receive it, if the Lord thinks it is good for me."

Kristian Primdahl is thirty years old, and was adopted by a Danish family in 1971 when he was eighteen months old. He now attends the Pentecostal church in Århus – and has also recounted his healing in a web page which gathers accounts of well-documented miracles.[2]

Notes:
1 Kristian Primdahl told his story in *Udfordringen* no. 4 - 25 January 2001
2 The address of the web page is: www.mirakler.dk
Photos from the TV program used with the kind permission of Angel Production.

# 11,000 in Copenhagen

**The meetings were extended two days due to the large number of people who stood outside every evening and couldn't get in.**

The next time Charles Ndifon came to Denmark was at the Copenhagen Christian Culture Center (CCCC) at Nørrebro. And now a lot more people knew about the healer due to the "Supernatural Powers" programs in the autumn of 2000.

The meetings with Ndifon in CCCC took place in February 2001, and more than eleven thousand people came along! The meetings were extended two days due to the large number of people who stood outside every evening and couldn't get in.

Journalist Bodil Harild, who used to work for Kristeligt Dagblad (a Christian daily newspaper), was at the scene and described the atmosphere:[1]

"The first people already began to arrive at around 3:00 pm, even though the evening meetings only began at 7:00 pm. On Saturday night the meeting went on until 2:00 am. Countless sick people came forward for prayer and were declared to have been healed by God. And Charles Ndifon gave them instructions on how they should continue to stay healthy."

## Lying on mattresses

"I arrived at the Copenhagen Christian Culture Center on Drejer Street more than an hour before the meeting with Charles Ndifon was due to start. But the large church hall was already almost full, and people were watching the events on a big screen in one of the other rooms.

Two sick women were lying on mattresses piled up with pillows in the very front row right under the podium. One had leukemia which had weakened her legs so much that she hadn't been able to walk for several months. The other had a very painful back problem which the doctors had also been unable to do anything about.

The entire front row in the middle had been reserved for wheelchair patients. The room was quivering with expectation. Mothers with sick children could be seen here and there.

Ndifon arrived some time later. He caught sight of the woman with leukemia lying at the front and to the side, in her den of despair.

'Are your ready' he asks suddenly with an earnest smile, and walks towards her. 'Are you ready to receive God's healing this evening?' The translator is busy translating, as the woman answers in English and tells of her illness. She bears the marks of having undergone chemotherapy. Her body is clearly weak. She answers that she doesn't only want the miracle to happen, but also that she might avoid the illness recurring. This is exactly what Ndifon gave special instructions about and what he teaches on in the day meetings and also practices exhaustively.

There is almost a solid wall of expectation when he arrives. During the evening he preaches that the Holy Spirit is very powerfully present this very evening.

More than a thousand people stand with their arms raised or stretched out as he prays for healing… or commands healing to take place, which he says will happen when the spirit of sickness leave the person in Jesus' name.

## The doctors had promised her less than a year

A woman with lung cancer had come by train from Jutland on Wednesday.

"I have been told that I won't be here in 12 months, but I now know that I will be", she said into the microphone.

She was quite emaciated, and hadn't been able to conceive how she would physically manage to participate in the meetings, since she could never keep herself awake after 10:00 pm. But now she had taken part in all the meetings until 2:00 am in the morning and was convinced that a miracle had happened and that her illness was gone.

There were so many such testimonies. Charles Ndifon asked if there was anyone there who was deaf because they had lost an ear drum, and a man and a woman came forward. The man had a hearing aid on his right ear, but could not hear with his left ear.

Ndifon commanded the deaf spirit to leave him in Jesus name. He clapped loudly several times and spoke to him on his left side, but the deaf man answered that he could hear him with his right ear. Then his right ear was covered by the assistants, and the trial repeated. Suddenly the deaf man could hear with his left ear. Charles went behind him and across the floor, saying various words, while the newly healed man indicated that he heard him, put up his hand and indicated the number of claps by raising that number of fingers.

"Your ear drum was gone, but now new acoustic nerves are growing. God is almighty", said Ndifon, and thus it continued the rest of the evening.

Suddenly the sick woman got up from her bed and walked reservedly towards the podium. The hall rejoiced. Before long she started dancing.

She stayed there the whole evening, sitting and watching the others who were healed. She wanted to lie back down on her mattress, since she had naturally lost a lot of strength, but was told to reject the tiredness and sit on a chair beside her husband and family. She positively beamed with happiness. "God has healed me!"

One of Ndifon's assistants, minister and singer, Mark Cole, from Vancouver, Canada, wrote an email home to his family about this experience, and closed by saying:

"Even now it brings tears to my eyes when I remember that experience. She was completely healed of her lameness. Praise the Lord![2]

## But – what if it comes back?

"It's so easy", Ndifon kept saying. "The sick spirit has been planted by the Devil, send it away if it shows up again! Look at me! What do you think I would do if I began to develop symptoms of some illness or other? What do you think I would say?

'Wrong address, Devil, don't try that kind of thing on me!'"

And Ndifon illustrated using a very small gap between his thumb and forefinger, how small the Devil's power is before Jesus, God's son:

"The evil one has been conquered! It happened when Jesus died on the cross for sinners and conquered death."

In USA there is a senator who is ninety eight years old. He has just been re-elected and now has six active years as a senator ahead of him. Don't believe you are finished just because you turn sixty or seventy. The Lord needs you!

## Incredible account from Australia

Ndifon told the assembly that in Australia he had healed a woman who was blind. She came up to him and he asked her what she wanted from him.

"To see again with my left eye!" she said, and took out a glass eye. I said, "Do you believe that God can heal you?" "Yes", she answered.

"Get ready for your optical nerves to be regenerated!" said Ndifon. And suddenly the woman said, "I can see light", and her eye began to regenerate in her empty eye socket.

"Nothing is impossible for God! Just think about the fact that it's him that created everything! Shouldn't he be able to regenerate an eye or an ear drum and get the nerves to live again?" The audience gasped.

They did so again when he told of a small child that had been dead for almost a whole day and was brought to him. The little one was brought to life, and "What should I say, it wasn't me, it was God. It's Jesus' name that heals".

## Sublime atmosphere

People stood with their hands stretched up to heaven, and reached out as the countless healings took place.

"Bring all the children up here!", said Charles, and the mothers came forward, carrying their small children. One by one he dealt with them and hugged them. He carried a crying infant in his arms and it became quite calm and quiet. He asked the mothers what was wrong. A mother with a slightly

*Before a meeting in Norway*

bigger boy, who didn't have a single hair on his head, explained that it was a side effect from an illness in his immune defense system that made him, at eight years old, look like he had been tonsured.

Ndifon held the boy's head gently and said to his mother that in four to six weeks the hair would begin to grow normally again. Optimism and strong faith permeated the entire meeting in this way. I didn't see anyone go away disappointed.

As midnight approached, those in the neighboring room were called in, and one by one all the sick went up for the healing which apparently accompanied his words and faith.

Occasionally he used shock techniques – shouting suddenly and unexpectedly at the spirit of illness, so that people jumped. But there was no mistaking the effect. A man, who had not been able to walk that morning, ran up and down the stairs. Everyone with various forms of cancer was asked to speak about it, and Ndifon comforted them with these words, "Are you ready for God's healing now?". With their confirmation came the promise. God can do anything. God is almighty! Hallelujah! Diabetes, heart disease, high blood pressure, nothing was overlooked.

"There are three people here who have AIDS", he said, and one came forward and was promised healing. It's no wonder that these meetings were met with such overwhelming interest. Because if you are sick, only one thing counts: getting well again. And it is glorious to witness that", concluded Bodil Harild.

## Were they healed?

The question which naturally comes to mind for the sceptic who only hears about all these wonderful healings and was not actually there, is: Were they really healed? Doctor Tine Damsgaard was at a Ndifon meeting in CCCC, and carried out a superficial examination of those who experienced changes:

"Of course it's difficult to determine whether people have experienced complete healing without a thorough examination", says Tine Damsgaard.[3]

"But when people describe their diagnosis and explain what they are able to do with their bodies after Ndifon's prayer, there's no doubt that a positive change in their situation has taken place."

Jane had lung cancer in the terminal stage, and had therefore been given up on by the doctors. She described how after prayer last Friday she could run up and down stairs, and had also gone for a walk of several kilometers.

"You aren't normally able to do that with such an advanced degree of lung cancer", explains Tine Damsgaard. She encourages everyone who has experienced an improvement in their state of health to go to their doctor.

"The things which happen at these meetings are wonderful, and there is nothing wrong in getting a doctor to confirm the positive things which are happening", says Jarle Tangstad, who is a minister in the Pentecostal church.

However, many of those healed don't see a doctor afterwards – despite encouragement from both Ndifon and the arrangers – perhaps out of fear of being laughed at by a doctor who doesn't believe either in alternative treatment or God. The churches which arrange the meetings take neither an admission charge nor information about the visitors. It is completely up to the sick/healed whether they want contact with the churches afterwards and if they want to talk about their healing. Experience has shown that most prefer anonymity.

At CCCC, the attendees were asked to fill out a response card if they had experienced something and believed that they had been healed. Only a small percentage of those who were healed did this, around 200.

As we will see in a later chapter, statistics about some of those healed at CCCC have been gathered, and a large proportion had been genuinely healed when they were contacted six months later. But there is also a quite large proportion who "lose" their healing again, or who weren't actually healed after all. Why?

A minister from a Faroese free church put it like this:

"Ndifon searches single-mindedly for just the tiniest amount of faith in the people who are sick. Then he takes hold of this faith and heals them."

Ndifon proclaimed at the meetings in Copenhagen:

"I am neither a miracle-worker or healer. I am just a messenger from God who talks about what Jesus can do for people.

Ndifon thus denies that he has special abilities – he just helps people to grab hold of something which he claims is already available for Christians, but which they rarely use because they don't dare to believe in it.

Notes:
1 Used in *Udfordringen*, 1 March 2001, page 3.
2 Mark Cole in an email reproduced on Ndifon's web page: www.christlove.org
3 To KKR/TV, quoted on their web page: www.kkr-tv.dk shortly after the meetings.

# What did they experience?

**That Jesus is at the center in Charles Ndifon's healings is something you are left in no doubt about after being to his meetings...**

In contrast to many healers, Ndifon gives God all the glory for what happens. And although he now spends all his time traveling from country to country, healing the sick, Charles Ndifon repeats, time after time, that the biggest miracle for him to see is *to know Jesus*. Later in this book he describes in more detail how a personal vision of Jesus Christ many years ago, set him on the path to his now worldwide service.

Several others have also jubilantly expressed that "meeting Jesus" far exceeds any miracle they might have experienced.

But what does it mean 'to meet Jesus'? Didn't he die about two thousand years ago? And if he rose again, didn't he rise up to heaven and disappear in the clouds before his disciples' very eyes? How then can one talk about meeting him today in our modern society?

Here are some examples of what people who have "met Jesus" say after the meetings:[1]

## Minister's daughter doubted – but saw Jesus

Susanne (who wishes to remain anonymous) was one of those who were skeptical. She had grown up in a minister's family, but still had trouble believing. For the last several years she was a self-declared atheist.

During a Ndifon meeting, Susanne experienced a miracle which changed her life and attitude completely. Some years ago, Susanne gave birth to a son. During the birth her outer sphincter muscle in her rectum tore, and the surrounding nerves died. The doctors couldn't treat it, but suggested operating again after a few years. Since then Susanne has had to get used to living with the associated problems. One evening she saw the TV program on TV2 Zulu featuring Charles Ndifon, and decided to go and see him at the Copenhagen Christian Culture Center.

"The next day I was sitting at home alone in my lounge room, working. My husband and our son were not home. Suddenly a figure came walking by! It was Jesus. As he walked past he turned and looked straight at me. His gaze was full of love and strength. It hit me right in the heart, and I began to cry. I just couldn't stop, and I felt an incredible impulse to follow him.

Susanne decided after this experience to go to one more meeting with Charles Ndifon that evening.

"I felt like I'd been struck by lightning. It was violent. As I lay on the floor, I can remember that a lot of people were suddenly standing around me. Someone said it was God's power, and I should just let it happen. I could feel the dead nerves beginning to come back to life. It was fantastic!"

Susanne has been examined by her doctors and has been told that she doesn't need to be operated on again.

## Dorrit - a "closet Christian" comes out

Dorrit from Svendborg, together with a friend, had traveled a long way to see the charismatic Nigerian at the Copenhagen Christian Culture Center.

Dorrit had always been a "closet Christian", and as a former hippy, had experimented with many things in the spiritual universe.

"Friday evening was our first meeting, and we had come in good time to get something to eat in the cafe. But to our great surprise, we discovered that almost two thousand people already stood outside waiting to come in. We therefore thought it was best that we patiently stand in the queue."

"There was just so much good energy in that building", Dorrit recalls. "The atmosphere in the hall was wonderful, and there was such an air of expectation. I noticed that the atmosphere became even more powerful when the singers and musicians began to lead us in song. God simply came into the room. It was fantastic, something I have never experienced before", Dorrit explains. The whole thing was beautiful, from the time we stood in the queue and waited, until Ndifon began to speak.

## Jesus came surging in

As Charles began to speak it was if my heart opened up and Jesus came "surging" in. Jesus became living, he became close and personal to me; it was just indescribable. Charles Ndifon's way of talking about God was wonderful. He really knew how to portray Jesus' unconditional love in such a way that you really felt loved".

Copenhagen:
*"Thousands attend
healing meeting"*

"During the last meeting with Charles I suddenly became fearful that it would all disappear when I went home. I therefore asked Victoria, one of Ndifon's co-workers if she would pray for me. That helped. God gave me the ability to hold onto him, and I have had the most wonderful months in my life.

## A new fellowship

In July 2001 I was baptized and I now attend the Pentecostal church in Svendborg. I feel as if I have been cleansed, I have become happy and well-balanced. I have also become part of a fellowship which is unique. I still have a lot to learn, but I am on the right path."

"And I simply can't do without Charles' 'Jesus teaching'. I often sit and do yoga while I listen to the tapes from the meetings in Copenhagen.

"I just have to go to Copenhagen again", says Dorrit. "My girlfriend and I baked a lot of buns and sold them at the Langeland Island festival to get money for the trip. We have the money now, and I am looking forward to going to Copenhagen, just as much as if I was going on a holiday to the warm south", Dorrit concludes enthusiastically.

But Dorrit wasn't the only person who had gone to Copenhagen from Funen. A young girl who had been hard hit by multiple sclerosis traveled together with one of her five home caregivers to Copenhagen.

Note 1: Told to René Ottesen in *Korsets Evangelium*

# Henriette's story

**Henriette Kyster had been crippled by multiple sclerosis – but was healed in just a few minutes – and it is still lasting one year later**

One bright sunny day in February 2002 I met the now twenty seven year-old Henriette Kyster in Odense. She came walking up briskly, and it was hard to imagine that just twelve months ago Henriette was so sick that she had to have four to five caregivers during the day in order to manage.

"I needed help with everything. When I got up, when I had a shower, when I had to go to the toilet, when I ate…

Without the caregivers I was fairly helpless", explains Henriette.

## The football girl was taken off the team

"It all began in 1995. I played football four times a week and loved sport. Suddenly I began to lose my balance and my legs went to sleep.

In January 1996 I underwent a number of intensive examinations at Odense University Hospital, and it was found that I had multiple sclerosis! After that it all went downhill quickly. I had one 'attack' after another, and was pumped full of medicine", Henriette recalls, who was twenty one years old at the time.

"First I had to use a walking stick, then a walking frame, and in the summer of 1996 I had to have a wheelchair. I was constantly in and out of hospital, went to futile rehabilitation in Ringe and got worse and worse. In 1998 I couldn't use either my arms or legs. When I wanted to smoke I had to use a smoking robot…!"

## Distressed mother

Henriette's mother, Käte Caspersen remembers that period as a living nightmare.

"I was completely knocked out. What had happened to our girl who was so full of life?" she asked herself. "But when they began to talk about a care center and a room with an eighty year-old neighbor on one side and a ninety year-old on the other, we said 'enough!' Fortunately things worked out so that Henriette could remain in her own home with extra help", explains Käte.

But Henriette wouldn't give up in the face of the dreadful disease:

"I fought like mad", says Henriette.

"I wasn't going to let that disease be the end of me, and after a while I did improve. In the end I could begin to walk with a walking stick in one hand, and a support person on the other side.

But I was still very dependent on help."

## "You're coming to the healing meeting, damn it!"

Henriette's mother had seen Charles Ndifon on the TV program "Supernatural Powers". They knew the person who in September 2000 had apparently stood up from their wheelchair at the first meetings in Ringkøbing – in front of the camera. Henriette's mother therefore began to talk with Henriette about the idea of her going to the meeting in Copenhagen in February.

"I didn't have much confidence in it", Henriette admits.

"'No, I'm not one for those hallelujah meetings', I said. But one of my personal carers from home care, Katja, banged on the table and said: 'You're coming to that healing meeting, damn it!'

She also promised to pay the bridge tolls, and come over with me in my modified car. So in the end I agreed."

Henriette Kyster was still very skeptical when she got to Copenhagen. Along with hundreds of others, she sat in a tightly packed side room to the meeting with Charles Ndifon. There was not enough room in the actual hall of the Copenhagen Christian Culture Center, but the meeting was broadcast on a big screen in a smaller room.

Because of the TV program, "Supernatural Powers", so many people wanted to meet this "Christian healer", that hundreds missed out every evening. Two thousand four hundred people sat inside every evening. There were a total of over ten thousand visitors to CCCC that week in February. The center is located in a big building on Drejer street in Nørrebro, which had earlier belonged to the workers' movement.

## A cigarette or Ndifon

"The atmosphere was tremendous, and you were on a real high, but even so, I still had lots of doubts. This is just too far out, I thought. When they began to pray for people in wheelchairs and they got up out of their wheelchairs, I thought: 'They must've been given a lot of money to do that.'

"Most of all I wanted to go outside and smoke a cigarette", recalls Henriette.

"But Katja thought I should try going forward for prayer: 'Now we've come all the way to Copenhagen from Odense, you can at least try being prayed for.'

'OK, that's all right', I said.

## The healing happened as I walked...

"When they began to pray for me, something weird happened: Something like an electric shock ran through me, and I burst into tears. It was if someone had turned on a switch. There were two to three helpers who tried to help get me on my feet. Suddenly I heard a voice say: 'Move out of the way, just let her walk – she can do it herself.' They let go of me, and I discovered that there was now only one person who held me with one finger.

I threw down my walking stick and walked. At first my legs and arms waved about like drum sticks, but slowly they became more sure."

"I just cried and cried... It was unbelievable. It was what I had dreamt about for many years.

*Henriette in her wheelchair before the healing: Without my 4-5 helpers I was fairly helpless"*

47

Then the helpers told me that I should go over to the hall where Ndifon was and tell them that I could walk again.

I walked –and it turned out to be quite a long trip; I went up the stairs in the Pentecostal church, I walked around in the aisles and up on the stage, where hundreds of people applauded me. It was absolutely fantastic! And as I walked that distance, I could walk better and better…

When I arrived, I was completely healed.

## "I gave my mother a big surprise!"

"In the middle of the night we drove back to Odense again. We were very tired and my friend slept at my place.

When I woke up the next morning I remembered everything I had experienced, and I didn't dare get out of bed. Imagine if I hadn't gotten better after all. I lay there for hours and tried to feel. But I could feel that my legs were well.

Finally I was so desperate to go to the toilet that I had to get up, and when my legs touched the floor, they worked.

Mid-morning my mother rang. She would really have liked to have gone along to the meeting in Copenhagen but had not been able to:

'Well, did anything happen over there?' she asked cautiously. I decided to really give her a big surprise. So instead of telling her about what had actually happened, I said:

'No, I'm afraid I have to disappoint you there. Nothing really happened…'

'Oh well, at least you've tried now', she comforted."

## Played football and climbed in the trees

Shortly afterwards Käte saw her daughter come walking towards her. She was completely overwhelmed and cried with joy.

"I almost couldn't believe my own eyes. It was so absolutely unbelievable. I was just as happy to see her walking as the time she took her first step. And I remember that Henriette didn't want to sit down. She wanted to be on her feet the whole time."

"Yes I walked the whole day that Sunday", recalls Henriette. "The next day I played football with my nephew and climbed trees with him!

And now I ride my bicycle and do everything I want to. You don't know how much you can miss riding a bicycle…!"

Henriette also went on her first trip alone – to Greece.

"I could go out again. I could run... I have had heaps of good experiences in the year that has passed since the healing.

## The doctors had trouble believing it

"The doctors rejoice in what has happened to me, but they don't recognize it as a miracle. They say that it would no doubt have happened anyway... But that's absolutely crazy – why should I 'coincidentally' get well on precisely that evening?", notes Henriette, and adds bluntly:

"I don't give a damn what the doctors say. People can believe it was trickery if they want to, but I know something happened that got me walking again.

Initially Henriette continued to have checkups and took medication to prevent the symptoms from developing again.

"When I am stressed, I can get a bit dizzy or feel a tingling in my legs. But

*Previously, Henriette had to use a specially-modified vehicle with a lift for her wheelchair. Here she is in summer 2001, without crutches or wheelchair – inexplicably healed in just a few seconds.*

*"I was just as happy to see her walking as the time she took her first step", says Henriette's mother Kate Thomsen.*

there are other people who experience that kind of thing. And it's getting less and less."

## How much faith is necessary to get healed...?

Henriette didn't have much confidence in it – but it happened anyway. And in the first year after the healing, Henriette also had difficulty actually believing in a good God, "Where was He all the years when everything fell to pieces", she thought. But on the other hand, she has become convinced that "there is more between heaven and earth…". When Charles Ndifon came to Odense again in February 2002, she went out to eat with him:

"Charles is a lot of fun, so there was lot's of fooling around", she says.

"I think by now I have been given answers to some of my questions. It is true that I had lots of questions about God and Christianity in the beginning, but in this week where I have been along to the meetings, I have decided that it's the road I will take. I want to believe in Jesus, and I'm sure that He will give me answers along the way to all the questions I have.

"My father still has trouble believing that it was God who did it. So we don't talk much about it. But now my mother is also coming to church."

# Physiotherapist's slipped disc healed

**Hanne Kirschheiner had the beginnings of a slipped disc, but "sacrificed" a family evening to go to an Ndifon meeting – and could do "impossible" back exercises afterwards.**

"Thursday, September 20, 2001 I had been looking forward to a relaxing evening at home with my family – finally an evening where I didn't have anything I had to do. But it ended up being a different kind of evening off – and my family had to manage at home alone", says Hanne Kirschheiner:[1]

"I am 43 years old, and a physiotherapist. Over the previous six months I had suffered from throbbing pain and tingling in my left leg. After the summer holiday it got much worse, especially in my foot, and I also began to notice that I had pain in my lower back when I rode my bicycle. During August the symptoms got worse and I began to have trouble falling asleep due to lower back pain and pain in my leg.

"On August 22nd I therefore asked the head doctor in the department where I worked to examine me. She examined me and referred me for x-ray and to a physiotherapist. Luckily the x-ray showed no abnormalities. The result of all the examinations was that I appeared to have the beginnings of a slipped disc, low in my lumbar region, which was pinching a nerve, and that my leg pain was thus sciatica pain.

## I couldn't sit

"I was instructed in how to do exercises several times a day, where I had to sway around a lot in my lumbar region. I also had to be careful not to bend over forwards, and to keep my lower back rigid when I sat down, stood up, etc. For nearly two weeks I couldn't sit down at all.

"It was impossible to sleep through a whole night. Despite a firmer mattress and a cushion for my stomach/lumbar, I couldn't lie down without

51

experiencing pain. This didn't get any better despite the exercises. However I began to be able to sit down if I sat in a rigid chair, ideally with a wedge-shaped cushion and a pillow behind my lumbar. I had been able to stand, walk and run the whole time. However, the pain in my leg increased if I walked for a long time, and my leg often felt clumsy and heavy, as if it didn't want to cooperate from my hip down.

## Healed in a different way

"During the whole period I had asked for prayer from friends. I had also – as the book of James talks about, asked the ministers in the Bethlehem Fellowship to anoint me with oil and pray for me. I therefore *believed* that God would heal me, but I expected it to happen gradually.

"Since there was a lady from our home group in Gentofte, Gerd, who really wanted to go in to the meetings with Charles Ndifon in the Copenhagen Christian Culture Center, and didn't want to go alone, I sacrificed my evening off with my family.

"I admit that I had wanted to meet Charles Ndifon ever since I had seen him on TV, but I didn't want to be healed myself at a large public meeting like that. I was afraid of having to stand in a queue, get pushed in my back, and especially of having to sit down for hours. And my worst fears were realized. I got worse and worse for each hour that passed. Even though I constantly walked out in the aisle and bent over backwards, in the end I could neither sit nor stand due to throbbing "toothache-like" pain through my pelvis and down to my left foot.

'We had better go home; you're not comfortable', Gerd concluded in the end. But we agreed to stay just a bit longer. Perhaps we might soon be able to go into the big hall – we were sitting in a side room and were watching everything on video.

## The pain was gone

"In the end, however, I felt a kind of hopelessness about it all. 'I could just as well have watched it all on TV', I thought. 'After all, I'm still only watching a video.' I actually also felt as if God had forgotten me.

"Then I heard Charles Ndifon say: 'I can sense that some people are beginning to be healed out in the rooms where they are watching on video.' I discovered that the pain was gone. My pain has never been constant. It has come and gone, so I couldn't be sure that there was anything unusual about

*Hanne Kirschheiner, a physiotherapist, and mother to Dorte (9) and Daniel (5), and married to Ole, who is a teacher. The family have been missionaries in Nepal for 11 years and have now started a house church – in a suburb of Copenhagen.*

it –although the pain had been insufferable until that point.

"Then the usher came and took us all into the hall where room had become available on the dress circle. Up in the dress circle I asked God, 'Honestly God, what are you doing with me?'. I grabbed my Bible, and it opened almost by itself to Isaiah 53: 'Surely He took up our infirmities'.

Until then, all the healings had been about shoulders, tumors and demons, and I felt that I couldn't burden God with my little back problem.

*One of the largest newspapers in Denmark, EKSTRA BLADET, ran a double-page article on the meetings with Ndifon in Copenhagen*

## Do the impossible!

"'Nothing is impossible for God', said Charles Ndifon.

'If you can't walk, then stand up and walk. If you stay sitting, you will never realise that you can walk. God will heal you, but you have to stand up

54

*The headline from 25 February 2001 reads: Miracles at Nørrebro. Nørrebro is the part of Copenhagen where the working class used to live.*

and do what you can't do.'

I thought about it a while. If I was to do what I couldn't do, I should bend over forwards with my legs straight and touch my toes. That was normally a sure way to bring back my symptoms when they had gone away temporarily.

I looked down at Charles Ndifon, who until then had seemed as if he had never heard of back complaints, and then he said:

'If you have a back problem, you should do this', and he bent over with his legs straight and touched his toes.

'The Holy Spirit! It must be the Holy Spirit. He is saying exactly what I had just thought', I reflected. 'Obedience', I thought. 'I have promised God full obedience, and now he is saying that I should bend over and tickle my toes. I looked down, it was a long way down. Slowly my hands slid down along my stiff legs, until they reached my feet, and then up again quickly.

## Gymnast on the podium

Down on the stage, Charles Ndifon said: 'You must do what you couldn't do, again – faster – keep doing it!' I bent down again and curved my back down to my toes, again and again and again. It must have looked like a new form of worship, and the elderly couple beside me stared at me intensely. Embarrassed, I began to explain, 'I had a slipped disc when I came, but it seems to have gone now...'

"I stopped, and tried to feel... No pain! Then I sat down and curved my back, pressed myself together into a ball. No symptoms.

'I should go down and say I have been healed', I thought, but resisted.

'Everyone who knows they have been healed should come down and tell us, so that others can be edified', said Ndifon. 'The Holy Spirit again', I thought, 'no way around it'.

A short time later I appeared on the stage as a gymnast with a specialty in touching my toes (an exercise which I as a physiotherapist should recommend that even people with healthy backs refrain from doing, since it is too hard on the back).

## Simple obedience...

Now three days later, I rejoice in God's loving, individual intervention. I also rejoice in having had three good nights' sleep; about having had a long jog without limping; about having cleaned up in my son's bedroom with him; and about being able to sit in all kinds of impossible positions.

I'm not good at having faith in God for anything, let alone for healing. But God didn't ask me to believe. He asked me to obey, and I am used to that through twenty eight years as a Christian, concludes Hanne Kirschheiner. She wrote down her account just three days after the meeting.

# 8,000 attended meetings

**In September of the same year Charles Ndifon was invited back to Denmark.**

Charles Ndifon continued his healing meetings around the world. One week he was in Norway, the next he was in Zimbabwe. From 19-27, September, 2001, Charles Ndifon preached and healed in three Danish cities: Copenhagen – Kolding – Odense. And interest was still very great: He began with four days in Copenhagen, where more than eight thousand people took part in the meetings in the Copenhagen Christian Culture Center in Drejer Street. Again, many were healed.

In other countries where people are used to mass meetings, 8,000 might not sound like much. But for the Danish free churches it is quite exceptional to be able to attract so many people. And most of those who came were presumably non-churchgoers. An artery had been hit. Here was suddenly something which could appeal to the non-religious Danes, many of whom only come to church twice in their lives, even though they are members: when they are baptized and when they are buried. Both times they have to be carried in. But here they found that there was power behind the words.

Below is a sample of some of the healings, big and small: [1]

## Girl suddenly sees clearly!

A girl who normally never goes to church had heard about Charles Ndifon. She had suffered from severe vision impairment for many years which meant that she was unable to read. During the Friday meeting she went forward to be prayed for. She felt the characteristic inner heat which many experience during the prayer. She also felt that something happened inside her eyes. An employee from the Pentecostal church found her walking around in the Culture Center foyer, jubilantly reading signs…!

## Hearing impaired woman could hear.

A woman told how ten years ago someone threw some explosive fireworks in her face, destroying her hearing. She had gotten used to wearing a specially constructed hearing aid. She had been to several Ndifon meetings.

Friday evening she stood up in front and was prayed for. Suddenly she could distinguish sound and speech from each other. She walked around crying, saying repeatedly, "I can hear clearly, I can hear clearly!"

## "How could one not believe?!"

A young man had come by with his girlfriend out of curiosity. He had seen how a leg grew out, and how several people with walking difficulties stood up from their wheelchairs.

"I saw the most fantastic things happen around me. How could one not believe?!" he said, when asked about his own faith.

## Healed of arthritis in the hip and other complications.

Artisan, Winnie Dolva from Bagsværd has given an account of her illness and healing story from the meetings in September 2001 for this book. She is now sixty two years old, and she explains:

"About fifteen years ago I fell down some stairs. I was admitted to Herlev Hospital, where they were most interested in sewing together the long laceration to my head, but did nothing about the pain in my pelvic region.

For several months I had difficulty walking and couldn't lie down. After a few years, my doctor referred me to a specialist, who had various x-rays taken, and it was discovered that I had broken my pelvis in several places, and these had fused incorrectly.

There wasn't really anything that could be done about it, but I was referred to a physiotherapist.

When you have pain in one place, you often strain other joints.

*Winnie Dolva is an artisan*

58

I had problems with my ankles, which became swollen and painful.

I asked to have the same physiotherapist that my husband had at Skodsborg, where you could also have rehabilitation in the heated pool.

During the worst periods, I went to the physiotherapist, Tom, twice a week. At other times there could be longer, between treatments.

In August last year, Tom said that I had now strained my hip for so long by walking incorrectly that I should have to expect to have a new hip.

## Skeptical towards Ndifon

"Then Charles Ndifon came to Copenhagen in September 2001. Even though I am a Christian, I had my doubts about whether I could be helped. After all, people had prayed for me before, without anything happening.

When I arrived, the hall was completely full, but there was just one seat in one of the adjacent rooms. When I saw the big screen on which we could follow what was happening in the hall, I was ready to leave again. But it was pouring with rain, so I might just as well stay there until it passed, I thought.

Then one miracle after another began to be shown on the screen. (Ndifon was followed around by two video cameras, so that the whole hall could follow him on a big screen). The first was a young girl with cancer. She had lung cancer, and when Charles Ndifon said that she was healed now, I didn't believe it in my spirit. Imagine giving her such expectations – but then came people in wheelchairs who could stand up.

My neighbor on one side said at that point: 'You feel embarrassed about taking up a seat with a bad shoulder after seeing this.'

We agreed that when God's power was so powerfully present, we didn't even need to go into the hall, but left the meeting in faith that God had healed us. I didn't feel that any physical improvement had taken place, but was still very uplifted after the meeting.

The day after, there was no pain, the swelling in my ankles was completely gone. I still went for treatment with Tom as arranged. He usually started by mobilizing my joints. This time he was quite amazed, because they 'slid like butter', as he put it. I told him the story of the whole meeting.

'Yes, yes', he said, 'but come again next week.'

I did, and was in even better physical shape than the last time.

'You don't need to come any more', he said.

I promised Tom that next time Charles Ndifon came to town I would take him along to the meeting."

## Kolding: 1,600 were touched

Congress Hall in Tønder Street in Kolding was full to the last seat with about eighteen hundred people. Even so, almost every evening, about 500 people stood outside who couldn't get in as Ndifon spoke and healed the sick from September, 23$^{rd}$-25$^{th}$.

Sunday evening, there were so many, that the leaders asked those who were NOT so sick to go home again, to make room for the most sick... !

In Kolding it was the Apostolic Church who organized the meetings, under the leadership of Finn Ravn Hansen. Finn also tried to follow up the roughly 1,600 response cards he received from people who were either healed or who had expressed that they now believed in Jesus.

"People come to meet a healer, but are rarely interested in a church", Finn Ravn Hansen has to concede.[2] "The eighteen hundred people who came to the hall every evening were not people from the congregation", he points out.

"Many don't want contact afterwards. We have to respect that. But sixteen hundred responded that they had either said yes to Jesus, were interested in an Alpha course, or that they wanted to hear about similar meetings. So it's only now that the real work begins. We will now arrange meetings with Hans Berntsen and others which we can offer these interested people.[3]

"About four hundred expressed in writing that they had been healed – just at the Kolding meetings. There were both big and small things. Many said that they felt a strong heat, after which their pain disappeared. Now they need to hold onto their healing and not slip back." In a later chapter we will look at a random selection of these four hundred who were touched by healing at Kolding in one way or another. Many came from far away.

## Lack of room in Odense

In Odense, interest was quite great beforehand. In addition to the TV series, Supernatural Powers, the Odense Weekly newspaper had described the miraculous healing of a young girl from Funen in Copenhagen. Her picture had been on the front page of the hundred and seven thousand copies of the newspaper, and the story filled two pages inside.[4]

The local Pentecostal minister, Jan Due-Christensen predicted serious space problems. The telephones rang incessantly, and he knew from Copenhagen and Kolding how great an interest there suddenly was in the country for the Nigerian healing evangelist. He therefore tried to rent a hall which could hold more than the roughly four hundred and fifty who can fit

*The large Congress Hall in Kolding was as packed as the fire department would allow - and five hundred people had to wait outside.*

in his own church. Only the St. Jørgen's Hall was available, and it could only hold nine hundred at a time. He therefore arranged a morning meeting in addition to the two planned evening meetings on the 26th and 27th of September, 2001.

Just as at the other places, many ended up standing outside in vain, because there simply wasn't room.

## Involuntary tremors disappeared

Kirsten Waade was one of those who came to the morning meeting:

She had followed the TV series, "Supernatural Powers" on TV2 Zulu. She had seen the program which was on Charles Ndifon's meeting in Ringkøbing, where Roger Pedersen was healed of double vision.

"I had a problem with my head. I had an involuntary tremor and was afraid that it might be Parkinson's disease", Kirsten Waade explains.

"I was examined by a doctor who fortunately confirmed that it wasn't Parkinson's disease, but what was it then? I was referred to a specialist – a neurologist – and had made an appointment. But then I heard about the meetings with Ndifon in September 2001. There were so many people that there wasn't room, so an extra meeting was held one Thursday, to which I came along.

"*Did you go along to be healed or to see what it was all about?*"

"I don't really know." "I had a strong feeling that I should go along to it", says Kirsten Waade.

"I have never been to healing meetings or anything similar before, but I have always believed that it was possible for God to heal people, just as there are lots of examples of healings in the Bible."

If you are a Christian, I think you have to believe that it's true, and I don't understand the fact that some Christians doubt that it can happen."

"*Would you describe yourself as a Christian?*"

"Yes I would", Kirsten answers. Kirsten works as a secretary in Fredens Church in Odense.

"*What happened there?*"

"I experienced a great heat in my body."

"*How?*"

"I think it must be something like the hot flashes during menopause. But since I'm only fourty three years old, it can't be that.

"*Did anything happen to your head?*"

"Yes, the involuntary tremors stopped immediately. I had been having quite bad tremors, but these stopped."

"*How are you now, roughly four months later?*"

"I am still well. I occasionally have small relapses, but nothing like before. When I have a relapse, I hold onto the fact that it is gone. And it disappears again. That was what Charles Ndifon strongly emphasized that we should do: Hold onto the fact that God had healed us. And in my case it has worked", says Kirsten Waade.

Notes:

1 www.pinsekirken.dk/cn.htm, read on 28 February 2002

2 Interview in *Udfordringen*, week 41, 11. 10. 2001

3 Hans Berntsen is the director of Volvo in Aalborg, but after a serious car accident he began to pray for the sick in his spare time. He now leads his own organization, Mission Danmark, which has this webpage: www.missiondanmark.dk

4 Henriette Kyster's story, which is also discussed in a later chapter.

# People are being healed all around me...

**Suddenly one began to hear of friends and acquaintances who had been healed at the meetings...**

My own daughter, Maj-Britt, came home from Charles Ndifon's meeting in Kolding on Monday – before I had been along myself – and told her skeptical parents that she had been healed!

Maj-Britt, eighteen years old, has had her legs measured by a doctor who found that one leg was about one and a half cm shorter than the other. She has therefore had to walk with an insole in one shoe, but has still had pain in her back.

Maj-Britt told us: "I had unusually bad pain in my back this evening when I arrived there with Stine from my class at school. When Charles said that we should lay hands on the sick place, I put my hands on my short leg – and believed very strongly that it would be healed. Shortly afterwards I could feel a kind of tingling in it, and I was straightened up on one side.

Afterwards I went up to the platform, as he had said you should if you felt a change. At the front, someone checked if it was true. Then I came up onto the stage. Charles asked what had happened.
He asked if it still hurt.

"Yes, a bit", I answered.

"Feel again", he said.

If I tried to feel it again, it was completely gone. Suddenly I didn't have any pain in my back at all.

When Maj-Britt came home that evening, she took the insole out of her shoe. She hasn't worn it since. And she hasn't had pain in

*Maj-Britt no longer suffers from back pain*

63

her back either, as she used to. She has since been to the doctor, who observed that her back still appears to be crooked. But Maj-Britt no longer suffers the pain she did before.

## A good friend was healed...

The next evening, my wife Birthe and I went along ourselves to the meeting with Ndifon. We were very much delayed, and only arrived after all of the five hundred people who couldn't get in had gone home again.

So we went straight in. There wasn't a single empty seat, but in the entrance we met one of my friends, Ole Søgaard Jørgensen, who let us stand and wait in the dress circle.

Ole was kicked badly in his right knee by a horse three years ago, so that both his cruciate ligaments were badly damaged. After a difficult operation, he lay for one and a half months at the sports clinic at Århus County Hospital, and then another one and a half months at Haderslev Hospital. After hundred days, he resumed working at the Sillerup Nursing Home, but continued to have physiotherapy without any great effect. His right knee still couldn't bend very much.

Ole Søgaard Jørgensen has studied theology at Århus, and was formerly the leader of Indre Mission (a conservative state church movement) in his town, Christiansfeld. So he wasn't one who normally attended the Apostolic

*Ole was kicked badly in his right knee by a horse three years ago. After a difficult operation, his right knee still couldn't bend very much. But after the meeting it could.*

Church, but he is a very helpful person, and Tuesday evening he was helping an apostolic friend, John, by being an usher in the Congress Hall and collecting response cards. And his helpfulness was rewarded...

"I hadn't even considered going forward for prayer", explains Ole Søgaard. "But suddenly Charles Ndifon pointed up in the dress circle, where I stood, and said that there was someone there who had a damaged right knee that Jesus was going to heal. I knew it had to be me. Especially since he said *right* knee.

Charles then called forward the people who had been healed. I went down and stood in the queue, but couldn't feel anything.

When Charles came past and asked: 'Did it help?', I answered: 'It's certainly better than before...' "he smiled, and immediately something happened. Suddenly I could bend my leg about twenty degrees more", says Ole.

## Reflexologist was healed...

Ole's neighbor, Margit Weidmann, who is a reflexologist, by chance also came to the meetings. Some time ago Margit had to give up her alternative medicine practice in town because she had suffered bad whiplash in her neck. Eventually this developed into a lump.

Margit hadn't intended to go forward either, she was just professionally interested in this alternative form of healing. Besides, she was sitting behind all the wheelchairs, and thought that they should be dealt with first. But suddenly Charles Ndifon pointed in her direction and said that someone was sitting there with whiplash.

So she went up, and when he touched her, she was suddenly healed. And the lump in her neck disappeared as well... Margit has since followed an Alpha course, in order to find out more about Christianity.

Ole also saw another acquaintance from town. He went up together with Ole because his *left* leg was bad. But since it was initially only those who were called who were meant to go up, he was stopped by the assistants. However he was allowed to slip through anyway, because helpful Ole convinced the assistants. But nothing happened to this man's leg.

## My work colleague's mother was also healed...

At the place where I work, our graphic designer, Britt L. Skov, told us that her mother had also been healed at Ndifon's meetings:

I rang her mother, Joan Lønnecker, and was given this account:

"I have always had a bad back, and for many years I have awoken every night at about 2 am because of pain.

Then I have had to sit up with pillows behind my back and try to sleep on them", said Joan. The method has worked for many years, but is hard on my lower back. Joan has been able to manage her job at the Danish Postal Service where she is employed in Customer Service.

"But it has been hard, since I didn't sleep properly. And I also had problems bending over a desk when I was standing.

I actually went along to the meeting in Kolding because my sister is sick. As we stood there, Charles Ndifon said that if we were sick, we should lay hands on the sick place.

"Then the thought struck me that I was sick too, so I laid a hand on my back. Suddenly I felt a powerful heat in my whole body. It was as if I was on fire inside", says Joan.

"I don't know how long it lasted. But my sister's daughter, who was there too, also felt heat in her stomach, where she has had problems. And she is better now.

When I got home, I slept until the next morning, without problems. And since then I have slept well every night!

When I occasionally think that I can perhaps feel something, I remember that Charles said that we should pray for the illness to leave us in Jesus' name. And that's what I do. And it helps", says a very happy Joan Lønnecker.

Until a couple of years ago, Jane didn't know anything about "living Christianity". But then her daughter got a boyfriend who was an active Christian. Later the family followed, and Britt's parents are now involved in a small active church in Haderslev .

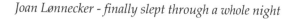

*Joan Lønnecker - finally slept through a whole night*

66

## Christina in the dumb waiter!

High school student, Christina Kobborg Andersen is another acquaintance, a twenty-year-old girl who was unlucky enough to get her fingers caught in a dumb waiter a few months before the meeting. She was stuck there for six hours, and she stood up – and sang – to help herself endure the pain!

The factory where she was cleaning was empty for the weekend, but fortunately she managed to signal someone outside the building by switching a light on and off. She was later rescued by Falck (Ambulance and Rescue Service) and treated at casualty. But some of her fingers remained numb.

When Charles Ndifon came to Kolding, Christina went along like so many others, to experience the meeting. She hadn't intended to be healed herself, but when Charles suggested that the sick lay hands on their sick places, she did it too.

"But I didn't feel anything", Christina recalls.

"Then when I got home I made a cup of tea – and burnt myself on the tea! That made me very happy: I knew I had regained feeling in my fingers!"

## Healed again!

On 16 March 2000 Christina experienced yet another healing!

It happened at a meeting with Volvo director, Hans Berntsen, in the Apostolic Church in Kolding, at which he prayed for many sick people.

"I have often had headaches and tension in my body, so I asked for prayer. When he looked at me, he noticed that one leg was longer than the other. He sat me on a chair with my back pressed against the seat. Hans Bernsten held both my ankles while he prayed, and he said I should watch what happened. My friend watched as well, and she, like me, could see that one leg grew about 5 cm as we watched! At the same time I could feel that something happened in my lower back, and immediately my headaches and tension were completely gone. I have been well ever since", says Christina.

*"Didn't he pull or push your legs?"*

"No, he just held them still, beside each other, so that I could see that one got longer…"

*Christina regained the feeling in her fingers*

67

# ZIMBABWE CRUSADE REPORT

## A NATION RIPEN UNTO HARVEST!

*Ndifon and his team have been in Zimbabwe several times - and the healings have been amazing*

68

# Healed of polio

...and other accounts from the Island of Funen,
from TV2 Funen and other sources

When she was one and a half years old, Hanne Mohr from Odense contracted Polio. She is now fifty five years old, and the polio has led to arthritis, back problems, a dislocated hip, and more than twenty five years with constant pain. But one evening in September 2001, Hanne's life was turned upside down. She went along to a meeting with Charles Ndifon, and God performed a miracle for her. Today Hanne lives a new life without pain:
"Every morning when I wake up I'm just so happy. My pain is gone. It's fantastic – so big that I lack the words to describe it", says Hanne.[1]

Eight years ago she had to give up her job as an office assistant in an export company. The pain was too great, and Hanne had to take early retirement. At that time she couldn't even walk 200 meters without having to stop and rest. Today she can go for walks and has begun to ride a bicycle.

"My son was a bit skeptical about the miracle at first, but then I asked him if he wanted me to take a run for him. When he saw me running happily around the lounge room, his eyes filled with tears. Now he could see that my pain was gone.

## I could suddenly run without pain

Hanne had seen Charles Ndifon in "Supernatural Powers" on TV2. Her physiotherapist told her that Ndifon was coming to Odense, and she decided to go to St. Jørgen's Hall to see him, along with her daughter. Hanne had a lot of pain that evening, but there was something else which preoccupied her.

"There was something special about the atmosphere that evening. I don't quite know how to explain it, but there was just such a special warmth and happiness in the hall. Both Ndifon and his co-workers radiated such a happiness.

However, as the evening raced on, Hanne had to lean more and more on her crutches, and the pain increased in her polio-affected left leg, and in her

69

hip and her back. Then Ndifon called her and others with similar pain forward.

"He said we should put a hand on the place that was sick. I sat down on a chair and held my leg. Then an assistant minister came and prayed for my leg. After the prayer, he asked me to get up and take a run with him. I got a shock when I suddenly realized I was running! It hurt a bit the first time, so the minister prayed for me again, and suddenly I was running around in the hall without any pain. From that point on I can't remember anymore, except that I got a big hug from Charles Ndifon – and otherwise just sat for a long time on a chair, staring straight ahead. I just couldn't comprehend it.

## Her daughter was also healed

The meeting in St. Jørgen's Hall was long, and it was 2.30 am before Hanne was sitting in her lounge room with her daughter, having a cup of coffee. They were both very happy, and Hanne ran around several times for her daughter at home. When she ran out into the hall, she discovered to her joy that yet another miracle had happened:

"I happened to look in the mirror. To my surprise I discovered that my dislocated hip was back in place again!

Hanne's twenty eight-year-old daughter was also healed at the meeting. She had dangerous cell alterations in her cervix, had been bleeding for a month leading up to the meeting, and might have needed an operation on her uterus. The day after the meeting in St. Jørgen's Hall, the bleeding stopped. Hanne says:

"At my daughter's next biopsy the doctor couldn't understand the good result. He said that there must be 'more between heaven and earth', but called her in for a new biopsy anyway, 'in case her cell test or journal had been swapped with someone else's by mistake'".

## A sunny story in the rain

Since her experience in St. Jørgen's Hall, Hanne has been telling people far and wide about her healing.

"I just can't help myself. It's so fantastic. I tell everyone who wants to hear about it – and most do. The other day I was out walking in the rain. I met a neighbor and asked: 'Do you want to hear a sunny story on a dreary day?' She did, and even though it was pouring down, I stood there for half an hour and told her my story."

Her new life has given Hanne a new face. "You can't hide it when you have pain – and there are many who say that I look different now. The other day, my six-year-old grandchild said to me: 'Grandma, it's like you don't have as many wrinkles on your face any more.'

Wrinkles or not, I certainly know that I am much more happy and thankful today. I also used to believe there was a God before. Now faith has become more real to me – and not a day passes in which I don't thank the Lord for my new life free of pain.

## Spiritual and psychological forces

"Even people who are not healed often feel that they have been helped."

That's the experience pastor Jan Due-Christensen has after the meetings with Charles Ndifon in association with the Pentecostal church in Odense.

*- Psychological forces can cause some to feel they have been healed, even though in reality they haven't been", believes Jan Due-Christensen.*

"Originally I was actually against inviting Charles Ndifon here to Odense", admits Jan Due-Christensen.

"I didn't want to risk some people being disappointed because they were not healed. As a minister you also feel a shepherd's responsibility for the people you are dealing with. And one has theological concerns about whether what is being preached really is appropriate.

But then I met some people from our town who had been along to the meetings in Copenhagen. They hadn't been healed, but they were happy…

They had had a positive experience. They had experienced God's spirit – they had heard about Jesus. And they had therefore improved anyway. Then I understood that I had worried myself unnecessarily on behalf of others.

## Big African faith

There is no doubt that Charles Ndifon has a big, bold faith. He has chosen to trust in God for everything. He grew up in Nigeria, where in many cases people have been forced to have faith in God because that was the only help there was. And then he also has an African spirituality which works as a

71

provocative and very refreshing injection into our church contexts, where we are often very intellectual in our relationship to God.

Charles fully and firmly believes that everyone can be healed, and that God will heal everyone if they just believe. Even though I myself no doubt have a less black and white conception of healing than Charles Ndifon, I believe that he is a God-given help to our people, which there is a need for right now. We therefore have to welcome him and accept his preaching, even though there might be subtleties which are left out. But I think we should use Charles Ndifon as an inspiration, not as a theological frame of reference.

If the people who come to the meetings just attend a Christian congregation afterwards, the problems can be managed. Then ministers can easily preach the other things and provide the everyday pastoral care which is necessary afterwards.

## Psychological powers also in play

*"Some are apparently healed, but afterwards their healing lapses. Why?"*

"The problem with healings which apparently 'recur' again after some time can be hard to understand. Ndifon would no doubt say that it's because we don't believe. I personally believe that in many cases what we see is a psychological effect at the meetings which is acting alongside God's power. Even though the preaching is about Jesus and power in his name, an atmosphere easily develops at a big meeting which puts some psychological forces into play.

We know, after all, that there are some euphoriants in the body which can make us feel certain things. And I believe that it is often these psychological forces which cause some to feel they have been healed, even though in reality they haven't been", believes Jan Due-Christensen.

## TV2 Funen on healing

TV2 Funen broadcast in October 2001 a program in the series "The Quarter Hour", on "Healing – fact or fiction?". The program was partly about Nielss Frederik Haagen Nielsen from Villestofte, Odense, who was diagnosed with multiple sclerosis ten years ago. Nielss won't accept that he is incurably ill. He has therefore experimented with alternative treatments:

"Bioacoustics, reflexology, healing, cranio-sacral healing, lying in a pyramid down at the border", he explains.

*"Has any of that worked?"*, asks the interviewer, Gitte Høxbroe.

"No", he answers tiredly after a short pause.

Nielss saw Ndifon on "Supernatural Powers" from Ringkøbing. "When I saw it, I thought, "Something is happening there! I want to meet him."

So Nielss went to St. Jørgen's Hall in Odense. No physical healing happened, but he became open to the spiritual, he says. When one of the assistants prayed for him, he experienced "the strongest thing I have ever experienced". It nearly makes my cry again to think of it, because I didn't then – not while it was happening, as he prayed, but afterwards", he says.

*Nielss is interviewed on TV2Fyn*

I spoke with Nielss in March 2002. He has now begun to attend the Pentecostal church in Odense, while continuing to experiment with alternative treatments. His wife is a kinesiologist, and he has been to Aalborg and believes he has been further helped by an Australian healer. On the other hand, he has lost faith in the public health system:

"When I went for a check-up at the hospital, the head doctor sat behind his desk – he didn't even touch me. Instead he offered to refer me to a psychologist. I accepted the offer, but it was a waste of time", says Nielss.

## Nursing assistant, Naja, was healed herself

Naja Hansen went along to one of Ndifon's meetings because she is a personal carer for a severely disabled man, but suddenly something happened and Ndifon called her forward.

"What happened?" Ndifon asked her (this was filmed and shown later in the TV segment).

"Everything disappeared suddenly", she answered tearfully.

Later she explains to the viewers with a big smile:

"I was virtually sucked to the floor, sucked backwards. It wasn't uncomfortable, it wasn't as if someone took me by the neck and pulled me to the floor. I was sucked to the floor, and it was very comfortable. But at the same time, my back hurt so much. It was crazy how much it hurt, and I howled. I was completely gone. Then he came and looked down at me and then – while they were trying to help me up, I saw such a giant light in front of me, and I became so light, and I have virtually flown around ever since", laughs Naja Hansen, who had serious back problems before.

## No more joking around

When TV2 Funen spoke with Naja Hansen, it was one month since she had experienced the healing in September 2001. The interviewer asked her how she was now.

"Well, I feel wonderful", she answered. Then Naja pulls up her shirt and displays her back, and the interviewer explains:

"Today there are only two scars left to witness to two breaks to the spine, arthritis and a slipped disc." And Naja continues:

"Before I used to sometimes make fun of that religion – with God and Jesus etc. I am very careful what I say now. It's not as if I go around praying and doing things like that, or go to church every Sunday – I don't. But it has changed my view of that religion."

*"How?"*

"I would say I respect the people who have that faith. And I won't make fun of them as I used to do before."

## Different reaction

There was another person on the program who had been to a Ndifon meeting and had not been healed, and who was now very displeased. That was Erling Skov, who works at Odense Teacher's College. He went to Copenhagen to be healed, but it didn't happen. He says in the program that it surpasses everything he has previously experienced in terms of irresponsibility and hysteria, because Charles Ndifon promises people that they can be healed. He suffers from a back complaint, but was not healed. On the contrary, according to him it got worse.

We will return later in the book to the problem of people who are not healed.

Note 1 To Louise Ø. Poulsen in an interview in the Pentecostal movement's magazine, KE, December 2001.
Note 2 TV clip used by permission from Director Ove Mulvad, TV2 Funen

# Is something unusual happening in Denmark?

Ndifon preaches and heals the sick in Jesus name all over the world. Oddly enough, he has met a special openness in Denmark – one of the most secular countries in the world. Is it a coincidence?

In February, Charles Ndifon suddenly popped up again in Denmark – this time in Odense, Denmark's third largest city. The organizers in Odense had planned a later meeting, but they were suddenly told that Ndifon wanted to come earlier, and they jumped at the offer.

"In fact, Ndifon particularly wanted to come back to Odense, because the people here were particularly important to him", explains Jan Due-Christensen. When Danes hear others say something so positive about us, our national modesty automatically comes into play. We have told ourselves and each other so often that "we're nothing special". We have trouble believing that someone, with no ulterior motive, would want to spend time with us, or that Denmark could mean something for other countries. Let alone something for God... But perhaps we are mistaken?

## Is what is happening in Denmark anything unusual?

When you read and hear about what is happening at Charles Ndifon's meetings in other places in the world, you have to go as far as Africa and Asia to see the same kind of large numbers of healings, as have happened in Denmark over the last couple of years during Charles Ndifon's visits.

Even though Australia, for example, has experienced some strong Christian revivals over the last ten years, people have not experienced as many miracles as have happened in Denmark.

The situation is Denmark is clearly something unusual, even though many have not yet appreciated that fact.

The foreign assistants who have taken part in Charles Ndifon's meetings in Denmark write home with excitement about everything which is happening. Michael B. Smith, an American who came along to the first February campaign in Copenhagen in 2001, wrote enthusiastically about the meetings in CCCC in an email which was reproduced on Ndifon's webpage.

He was particularly impressed by the fact that "at least eighty five per cent" of those attending were "unsaved". He bases this assessment on the fact that the majority stand up when Ndifon asks those who want to follow Jesus to stand up. Over seven thousand "stood up for Jesus" in Copenhagen in February.

People are apparently not used to that reaction in the USA, where many people at the meetings consider themselves to be conscious believers, born-again, filled with the Spirit, etc. – they don't need to receive Jesus – again.

Michael B. Smith comments that it is impossible to ask the non-believers to "come down to the altar", as they normally do in the USA. Because there isn't room for one thousand out of seventeen hundred to come forward!

He also talks about an excursion with Charles and half the team to Holbæk on Sunday morning, where they attended the service in the small church there. Normally fifty come, now there are six hundred, and about one hundred can't get inside...

## Prophecy about Denmark?

Back in Copenhagen he writes an email home from the office upstairs, while there is a meeting taking place in the hall:

*"I can hear Mark Cole from Vancouver, Canada, playing 'Great Is Thy Faithfulness' on the keyboard again this evening. That song makes it hard for me, as I would really like to go down and be part of the meeting. This song seems to be becoming a theme song for Denmark."*

And then he continues in prophetic style, as if he has received something from above:

*"Denmark, you are a burning light to Europe and this flame will not go out. From this place I will cause a flame to be spread across this Nation and spill to others as well. You were once part of the fierce Vikings taking the sword everywhere, but now I have given you a different sword with which to fight.*

*The fear on the enemy you once brought, shall be on those demonic spirits that bind my people when they hear of your coming. For I shall have a free people and you shall have a part."*

*"We need revival in the old movements and in the churches. And we need to reach people outside the churches," says pastor Jørgen Christensen (with the Bible).*

Time will tell whether it was a genuine prophecy Michael B. Smith wrote down about Denmark that evening.

## Waves of healing on Bornholm

Denmark has a special place in Charles Ndifon's heart in any case. From Sunday January 20, 2002 he was suddenly in Bornholm – a remote Danish rocky island south of Sweden and not far from Russia. The island was actually occupied by the Russians after the Second World War for a short period of time, but miraculously escaped from being incorporated into the communist Soviet Union. Perhaps this is because so many Christians on Bornholm prayed for their island. Bornholm has always had many more Christian believers than the rest of the country. But the old revival movements have slowly stiffened into orthodoxy. We will return to Bornholm later.

From Sunday morning through to Thursday evening he sought to heal everyone who wanted to be healed. And apparently hundreds of people received some form of healing or another.

There weren't many people in the rest of the country who noticed, but it clearly left its mark on Bornholm. This time it was the Pentecostal church in Rønne, which organized the meeting and recently invested in a hall for its meetings. Charles Ndifon is following in the footsteps of other healing preachers who have also visited the church and the island recently. Hans Berntsen, evangelist Josephine from Rwanda, and Christian Hedegaard (whose book "Victory Over Demons" was distributed to all households on the island). It has begun to cause a "shift" in the habitual religiosity.

## A renewed, spiritual powerhouse?

"We can feel that things are beginning to shift", says Jørgen Christensen, the Pentecostal minister, who moved to Bornholm with his locally-born wife two years ago. He has formerly been a leader in Copenhagen and other areas.

"Bornholm is the place from which the revival movements have spread to the rest of Denmark. And some say that more evangelists have been sent out from Bornholm than from the capital.

"Church attendance is much higher on Bornholm than in the rest of the country; about ten per cent", says Jørgen Christensen.

"But we also need revival in the old movements and in the churches. We need to reach people outside the churches. That's why we arranged these meetings with speakers who can reach further out.

We already have contact with many new people. For example, a large group of former drug abusers are now coming to our church from the Minnesota center," says Jørgen Christensen.

He dreams that one day Bornholm will again become a spiritual powerhouse for the whole country.

## Likes Odense

Three weeks later Ndifon was in Odense.

Again it was fantastic to witness how Charles Ndifon could call complete strangers forward who had particular illnesses which he could describe without knowing the individuals.

And when they later came forward, one could confirm that there had been precisely one person present with exactly that special illness and that pain.

Later in the book Ndifon describes how he receives these "words of knowledge".

78

## A kiss from the model

In Odense, Ndifon called forward a woman who had a particular kind of pain. She turned out to be a very well-known model who has also been on a TV quiz show. Ndifon didn't have a clue who she was.

When she came forward, he healed her, and in gratitude she gave him a hug, which those who are healed very commonly do in their emotional state.

But this time Ndifon was also given a big kiss – no doubt because he happened to turn his head to the same side as the model when she tried to give him a hug.

After midnight, when the meeting was finally over, the minister, Jan Due-Christensen invited me to have supper in a back room, together with Charles and his assistants. It was very relaxed and a lot of funny stories were told. My teenage son John was also there, and Charles started to speak to him of his own initiative, and was very friendly and encouraging towards him, as he is towards everyone – regardless of how insignificant people are according to the Danish national sense of modesty.

Jan then told Charles that the woman who had kissed him was a very well-known model, "I bet there were lots of guys who would have liked to get a kiss from her", he laughed.

*It doesn't cost anything to be healed in Jesus name... So what do you do when you experience a miracle in your life? You hug the preacher!*

Charles immediately joined in on the joke, "What can I do? The women always hug me. When I come home from these meetings, Donna always says, "Where have you been? You've got lipstick all over your face!"

And then he added more seriously, "It is really a blessing in a marriage when you can trust each other completely."

## Great gratitude

In the Bible there is an account in which Jesus heals ten people, but only one out of ten comes back to say thank you. Christian healing is fundamentally free. Many non-churchgoers have trouble accepting this. They want to pay for being healed in advance, just like when they go to a healer, so they don't owe anyone anything. But it doesn't work like that when God is involved. It's not something you can buy. It is a gift which God seems to generously share out – to those he chooses. Not even Charles Ndifon can decide who will be healed. And even though many prefer to live quietly with their miracle, letters arrive regularly from people who were healed. Here is an email which Jan Due-Christensen received on 28 February 2002, after the meetings in Odense:

Dear Jan,

Thank you for your letter regarding the meetings with Charles Ndifon. I would like to take up your offer of being sent a New Testament. It was an incredible experience which I will never forget. I myself have been very well since I was at one of the meetings. I make sure I pray a prayer every day, and that has definitely helped.

I feel that my body has become completely new, and that my life is completely different to before. It's a bit difficult to explain, but it's a lovely feeling. I had back and hip problems which meant that I often couldn't walk. I had suffered from these for eight years. It was rare for me to have a day which was free of pain.

I feel wonderful now, which is just so lovely. I also thank Jesus every day, and will continue to do so.

Yours sincerely - NN

Notes:
1 Reference to "the sword of the spirit"
– often used in the Bible to refer to *the Word* and *God's word*.

# "It's so easy..."

**"Many religious Christians are paradoxically harder to heal", admits Charles Ndifon. "It is much easier with people who are spiritually seeking..."**

*"Are there any others who want to be healed?"* Charles Ndifon asks those gathered at the hall in Rønne, Bornholm.

It is late, and we are all tired, but Charles keeps going. More people come forward. He heals them one by one in Jesus' name.

Sometimes it is clear that a change has taken place – for example if someone can hear who couldn't hear before; at other times it is impossible to see if a person really has been healed of cancer or diabetes. In one case, a person with diabetes who was told that their diabetes had been healed did a test during the meeting and could report a significantly lower result.

Some people are easy to deal with, others have several illnesses which he has to tease out by questioning them. But many cases he can tell complete strangers what their problem is and how it happened. He can describe their internal fractures and the cause of their pain.

*"How do you do it?"* I asked.

"These are words of knowledge which God gives me", explains Charles, and appears to marvel at the fact that someone who is a Christian themselves can ask such a silly question. Then he explains:

"The Lord talks to me all the time, often in pictures. Words of knowledge are one of the gifts which are mentioned in the Bible[1] and which have been known and used in churches everywhere."

"Except perhaps in the Danish National Church...", I think to myself.

## "It's so easy..."

"There is someone here who has lung cancer", he says.

"There is someone here who has pain here under their right arm, you have suffered an injury. God heals you now." Often he just clicks his fingers, "You are healed. The illness has left you."

Often he adds, "You are free. Enjoy life! Begin to dream again!"

"Some people are disappointed that I don't shout and scream, but why should I do that? God isn't deaf. It's not my performance that heals people, it is faith in Jesus alone."

"It's too easy!" Charles often says when he meets a particularly difficult case. Among the thousands who have already been healed at his meetings around the world, there have been some quite hopeless cases. For example, a man with no eyes who wanted to see. And who ended up seeing…! according to Charles.

He therefore never doubts that God can heal a sick person. But often there are evil spirits which have to be cast out. And if they don't leave voluntarily, Charles commands the sick spirit to leave in a firm voice – and afterwards the sick person can hear or see or move without pain.

Often the person's eyes or ears have to get used to the new situation. Like the person from Bornholm who could only see partially in one eye, and had therefore gotten used to only using the other. Or a woman from Århus who had had double vision for thirty four years, and had therefore gotten used to seeing that way:

"I play tennis – I just used to play with two rackets and two balls at the same time…", she said at the time she was healed. She now had to teach her eyes not to focus in the sick way. She had brought her daughter along with her who had developed a growth illness, which meant she had to use crutches. Charles apparently healed them both.

## Like Jesus did at Bethsaida

According to Ndifon, healings often happen gradually or in several stages.

In Mark 8:22-26, even Jesus had to heal the blind man at Bethsaida in two stages, because after the first attempt he only saw "trees walking around".

Since the man was born blind, his brain had to first learn to decode the visual sensations. This state is called *agnosia*, and has only recently been proven by researchers.[2]

This discovery indirectly proves that Jesus really healed people, since neither Mark nor anyone else at that time could have known that people who receive their sight after an operation/miracle cannot "understand" what they see if they hadn't ever been able to see before.

Charles also mentions places in the New Testament where it is said of a healing that it happened "within the hour" in which Jesus spoke the word.[3]

*Charles Ndifon lifts the crutches from a 14-year-old girl who has just been healed of a growth disorder. Bornholm 2002.*

He understands this to mean that in some cases a healing took place over a period of time, e.g. an hour.

## Let's clean up this place

*"Are there any more?"* asks Charles. He keeps going towards his declared goal of praying for everyone who wants to be healed.

*"Let's clean up this place"*, he says humorously.

At one point he says, "Let's make Bornholm a cancer-free zone! Let's heal all those with cancer, so that people from the rest of the country come here simply to be healed." People applaud, even though they probably have doubts about whether it is possible. But Charles places no limits on his dreams: Because nothing is impossible for God.

If he didn't have to move on the following week, he would no doubt have seriously tried to eradicate cancer from the whole island. He works forty eight weeks a year running healing campaigns around the whole world.

"If you help me, we can be finished in ten minutes", he says, as midnight approaches. But more sick people continue to come forward, while many of those already healed leave after many hours at the meeting.

When Charles talks about the sick *helping* him, what he means is that if they are ready to believe and receive their healing without reservation, things will move fast. But things drag out if people don't quite dare to believe or have thoughts in their head which prevent the miracle:

## Religious people are often the worst...

"Many religious Christians are paradoxically harder to heal", admits Charles Ndifon. "It is much easier with people who are spiritually seeking. They don't have their heads full of incorrect theology about it probably being God's will for them to suffer. That they probably need to learn a lesson. That they honor God in their pitiful state – and other stuff like that.

Excuses! That kind of theology arises where the church doesn't understand how to use God's power. So people say:

'Sure, the Bible says that we should "heal the sick, raise the dead, cleanse those who have leprosy, drive out demons" (Matthew 10:8), BUT...'

There is always a BUT.

Then people interpret, and take into account what such-and-such a big name has said, instead of going back and seeing what the Bible says."

"God doesn't need to gain honor by letting his children suffer", maintains

Charles. "What father would want his children to suffer so that he could be honored? God's not that kind of father.

And he gains more honor from a person who is healed in Jesus name.

And does he need to let his children suffer to teach us a lesson? What lesson have you learned by not getting well even though Jesus says you should? These are all just excuses because the church doesn't dare to take Jesus at his word."

Charles Ndifon has no doubt that all sickness is an attempt by Satan to destroy God's creation. And he gets angry when someone wants to give God the blame for an illness.

"There is so much *religiosity* preventing people from being able to meet Jesus. People are tired of religion, they are tired of old churches which just give them theology without any spiritual life, but they are interested in *Jesus*. And he's interested in them!"

## Healing in groups

He often gathers together a group with the same affliction. For example, he might discover that there are several people with hip problems, and call them all together. He then heals them together, the whole group. Along the way, he picks individuals out, whom he questions to ensure that they have also been healed. It appears that the majority are healed.

"It is important that you react quickly when I pray for your illness", Charles admonishes the sick.

"*Immediately* do what you couldn't do before. If you can't bend over, then bend over. If you can't walk, then jump up and walk. If you can't move your neck, then move it. If you can't see, try to use your eyes.

It is important that you immediately act in faith", Charles points out.

He believes that one big reason why Christians don't always get well after praying to God about it is precisely because they don't act in faith on what they have prayed about. They expect God to send a miracle from heaven, but God wants us to receive in faith and act on his promises.

"You don't doubt his promise of salvation do you? You don't have any choice. You *have to* trust Jesus. In the same way, you have to trust the promises Jesus makes about healing if you want to be well."

## "Lady, you have cancer don't you?"

Sunday morning on Bornholm Charles Ndifon started healing too soon and immediately sick people swarmed forward so that he didn't have the chance to give the teaching he wanted to give on "preserving your health" against the attacks of the Devil.

He therefore began Sunday evening with teaching, and he spoke quickly, powerfully and with inspiration.

But even so, it wasn't long before he needed an example.

So he looked down into the hall and pointed at a random woman, about fifty years of age, whom he'd never seen before.

"Lady, you have cancer, isn't that true?" he asked in his polite African way.

Yes, it is. The lady has breast cancer and comes from Århus, as I discovered when talking to her afterwards. She traveled over here because the doctors have given up on her. She also tried out an alternative healer in addition to her doctor, to no effect, and come to Bornholm in the hope that Charles Ndifon could help her.

"Don't be afraid", he says compassionately as she comes up with tears in her eyes. In all his contact with the sick he expresses acceptance and love, and gives many hugs and smiles.

"I'm not afraid", she answers. "I'm just touched."

## It's about driving out the spirit of cancer

Charles now uses her illness as an example, and explains that as soon as the sick cancer spirit is driven from her body, the cancer cells will die.

He illustrates using the account in Mark's gospel, chapter 11:12-14, 19-26, about the fig tree which Jesus curses.

"As soon as Jesus cursed the tree, it died. But it was only the next day that Peter *saw* that it was withered", Charles points out.

"As soon as I cast out the spirit of cancer, the cancer cells will die. But some time will still pass before the harmful effects have left the body.

Charles is well aware that many white people call this kind of thing superstition.

Afterwards he tells me, "White people have often told us that what we believed about the spirits was superstition. They didn't know any better. But it wasn't superstition. We know what we're dealing with! There is *murder* taking place in the spiritual battle. And unless you are a spirit-filled Christian who can protect yourself under God's power, it can be quite dangerous to go to Africa.

This man can't see well with his left eye

Ndifon instructs him to hold a hand over his good eye and try to focus on and touch Ndifon's nose.

Yes, it works. There it is! There it is!

# Gradual healing

A young man in a wheelchair who is paralyzed from the waist down, is declared to be healed, and his helpers are told to train his legs. But even though his helpers try to get him on his feet, he apparently hasn't gained feeling in his legs.

After a few attempts, he sits back down in his wheelchair.

*"Are there any more who haven't yet been healed"*, asks Charles. The young man in the wheelchair catches his eye. Charles goes over to him and asks in detail where the paralysis actually is.

He tries pricking the man in various places. Slowly, sensation comes a small distance under his waist. A bit later he can feel sensation even further down.

Charles explains:

"It will continue like that as life slowly comes into the nerves again. You will probably be healed within a couple of days. You can help him by testing where he has feeling", says Charles to his friends, two young men standing behind the wheelchair.

One of them got his hearing back in one ear a short time ago...

Notes:

1 In the New Testament, in 1 Corinthians 12, you can read about the gifts which the Holy Spirit gives to believers. Verses 7-11 specifically mention some of the gifts, including *knowledge* and healing, "Now to each one the manifestation of the Spirit is given for the common good. To one there is given through the Spirit the message of wisdom, to another the message of *knowledge* by means of the same Spirit, to another faith by the same Spirit, to another gifts of healing by that one Spirit, to another miraculous powers, to another prophecy, to another distinguishing between spirits, to another speaking in different kinds of tongues, and to still another the interpretation of tongues. All these are the work of one and the same Spirit, and he gives them to each one, just as he determines.

2 See, for ex: Oliver Sacks: An Anthropologist on Mars, Knoff, A. A., New York, 1995.

3 John 4:53: Then the father realized that this was the exact time at which Jesus had said to him, "Your son will live." So he and all his household believed.

88

# Worldview overturned...

**Mariam Ghias, a midwife from Iran was sure that it was trickery, but was healed herself...**

Mariam Ghias, went to a healing meeting on February 14, 2002 out of curiosity. Her work colleagues had talked about miracles – but she was sure it was trickery, and that those "healed" were just paid actors.

But suddenly there was a man there who wasn't healed straight away – Mariam could recognize his back pain; it was the same pain she had suffered herself for many years – and then something began to happen...

"Have I been hypnotized – or what? Is this really happening? I don't understand..."

Mariam Ghias was deeply amazed.

She had gone along to one of the much discussed healing meetings at the Pentecostal church in Odense one Thursday morning.

"Of course I didn't believe that healings were actually taking place. That kind of thing can't happen. But I have a couple of colleagues who had talked about it, and I got curious", she said straight after the meeting.

## Worldview shaken...

Mariam is still in shock. Something has just happened a quarter of an hour ago which has completely shaken her worldview.

"It doesn't fit with what I have learned", she keeps repeating.

"Is this all true?" she asks her colleagues, Els Reekmans (originally from Belgium) and Maria Cederquist who is an active member of the Pentecostal church in Odense.

"Yes, it's true all right", they confirm. And we all have trouble holding back a smile, because we have rarely seen someone who was so astonished.

## Just acting

"I stood up in front and watched everything that happened", Mariam says.

The Nigerian evangelist, Charles Ndifon, had called everyone with back and shoulder problems up onto the platform to heal them one by one in Jesus' name.

And they were apparently all healed. The pain was gone.

"But I was sure that it had been arranged, and that those 'healed' were just actors", says Mariam.

When Charles Ndifon got to the last man in the row, he asked the man to lift his left arm. He didn't dare, because he had a slipped disc and a lot of pain. But Charles took the man's arm and lifted it.

"I could see on the man's face that it hurt. And I know that pain because I myself have a slipped disc and lots of pain."

## Political refugee

Mariam came to Denmark sixteen years ago as a refugee from Khomeini's atrocities in Iran.

She has had more than enough of fanatical religion, and when I ask her what her religion is, she shrugs her shoulders and doesn't really know what to answer. She is just a normal Dane, who doesn't really believe in anything.

She is married and has two boys and a girl who are twenty four, eighteen and ten years old respectively. She has worked as a midwife at Odense hospital most of the time she has been in Denmark. But ten years ago she suffered a slipped disc.

## Pain for 10 years

"I fell off a bike; that's no doubt what started it all. I was operated on in Aalborg, but it didn't help. I eventually developed arthritis, and was operated on again to have scar tissue removed. But I still had a lot of pain.

I continued to work, but only part time because of the pain", says Mariam.

"She has really dragged herself around at work", her colleagues add. As recently as last September she was again in hospital.

"What happened just before?" I asked.

"I could see that that man really had a slipped disc, like me. His pain was real."

"But then he was eventually healed?"

"Yes, Charles Ndifon got him to do some movements with his body which I knew would have to hurt."

*"What was it you suddenly shouted out?"*

"I asked the man, 'Do you really have no pain? How can you do that without it hurting?' I didn't understand it."

Mariam's spontaneous reaction caused a stir in the hall, because she was standing right in front of the platform and suddenly started talking to them.

"What's she saying?", asked Ndifon. The interpreter, Jan Due-Christensen, explained Mariam's astonishment to him.

Charles Ndifon then called up Mariam herself and healed her in Jesus name in a matter of seconds.

"I suddenly felt a strong heat in my back and throughout my body. And right now I can't feel any pain…", she says - still amazed.

*"Have I been hypnotised – or what?" asked midwife Mariam Ghias (center) her two colleges, Els Reekmans (left) from Belgium and Maria Cederquist. This picture was taken right after the healing.*

## Have I been hypnotized?

After the healing Mariam's friend helped her back to her seat, but it wasn't long before Mariam again began to loudly ask questions in astonishment:

"Have I been hypnotized – or what?"

Charles Ndifon couldn't hold back a laugh. He went resolutely down to Mariam and took her by the hand and asked her a series of questions to get her "feet back on the ground":

"What's your name? How old are you? How many children do you have?" Mariam could answer them all.

"You see, you haven't been hypnotized. You have been healed!", he said.

Shortly afterwards Mariam was interviewed by DR TV1. The report was used in the news on Thursday evening, 15 February 2002. Unfortunately the whole story wasn't told. Only a short segment with a very astonished Mariam who said she had felt a heat in her body and that she didn't understand:

"It doesn't fit with what I have learnt", she said, among other things.

*"What do you think your family will say?"* I asked her before she went home.

"They will no doubt be happy that their mother is well again."

*Charles Ndifon lifts up a child that has been healed.*

# Psychic healers looking for power

**Many alternative healers have been touched through the teaching of Charles Ndifon – and have found a greater power...**

A woman, very well-known throughout Belgium and the Netherlands as an alternative healer came to the crusade meetings in Eersel, the Netherlands in May 2001.

She has been sought after by various government officials and even the archbishop of the Catholic church for help. Not only is she an alternative healer, but she also teaches her craft at her center for alternative healing.

Being curious about the miracles taking place at Charles Ndifon's meetings, she decided to come and she brought a friend with her as well. Upon seeing the power of God demonstrated in miracles, signs and wonders, she immediately began to weep. She came to the front along with her friend where they were both healed and they each accepted Jesus as their personal Savior. She testified that she had dreamt about Charles Ndifon for two nights prior to the meetings.

## 50 psychic healers on parade

The next night she came with her entire healing center comprised of about fifty psychic healers! They paraded into the meeting carrying lighted candles. Because there was not enough room for everyone, people began to turn them away. Pastor Charles saw this from the platform and beckoned them to come and sit on the floor right in front of him. As he continued to preach the Gospel in simplicity, miracles broke out!

Charles began calling people by specific words of knowledge and they were instantly healed! The psychics saw the awesome power and love of Jesus and all of them began weeping! Every single one of them started to believe in Christ and all that were sick were healed! They knew now, that Jesus was the healer.                  93

## Tell me what to do!

After Charles left Eersel, his associate, Pastor Victor Emenike, continued the meetings. He went and visited the woman at her alternative healing center. Her child-like faith was apparent as she asked Victor what she needed to do next. Victor instructed her to remove all of the psychic paraphernalia. Immediately, she removed everything!

She then asked again what else she could do. He then told her to change the name of her center. Because the center was registered under that name, she could not change it, but she happily added "Jesus is the healer!"

Since the meetings, she has been ministering to people in the name of Jesus and people are getting miraculously saved and healed! She has given herself whole-heartedly to Jesus.

## Religious people misunderstood

Her story actually begins, however, back when she was a teenager. She was orphaned at a very young age and was kept in various homes. As a teenager, she had a visitation. Suddenly, she saw a very bright light, but she did not know what it was.

She found some Christians and asked them what it could be. They told her that it was the devil. Shortly after that, she had another visitation with the same bright light, only this time, there was also a rainbow. Again, religious people told her that it was the devil. She had no one to explain to her what the light was, so she turned to spiritism.

Religious people had turned her away from Jesus, Charles explains. His associate, Victor Emenike, showed the lady scriptures from the Bible telling also about a great light:

The same thing happened to Saul on the road to Damascus. Acts 9:3 says that suddenly a bright light shone around him. That was the glory of God which he saw! In John 1:1-9, it explains that in Jesus is life and the life was the light of men. It goes on to say that Jesus is the true Light. Also, 1 John 1:5 states that God is light and there is no darkness in Him at all.

When Pastor Victor showed her these scriptures and others like them, she began to weep for now she knew that it was Jesus who had come to her.

## Lights and rainbows in the Bible

She then explained to Pastor Victor that on that first night of the meetings, she saw that same bright light all around Charles that she saw as a teenager. She said that it lit up the entire stage! She also testified that when Charles was giving words of knowledge for people to be healed, she saw the rainbow. She then knew that Jesus is real. When she saw the rainbow, she was healed.

The rainbow is found throughout the Bible when describing the presence of God. In Genesis 9:12-16, the rainbow was given as a sign of God's promise to Noah and all his descendants. Ezekiel also had a visitation from the Lord in Ezekiel 1:26-28. He describes God by saying that there was brightness all around and the appearance of a rainbow. Also, Revelation 4:3 states that there is a rainbow round about the throne of God, and in Revelation 10:1, John describes the appearance of a mighty angel who had a rainbow upon his head and his face shone like the sun.

This clearly authenticates this woman's experience, says Charles.

This former psychic alternative healer is now preaching Jesus Christ alive with signs and wonders following!! Glory to God! She is not alone. There are several former psychics in Denmark who have also dedicated their lives to telling others about Jesus. We serve an awesome God full of mercy and love!

*Charles Ndifon preached the good news of salvation when he was visiting India in 2000.*

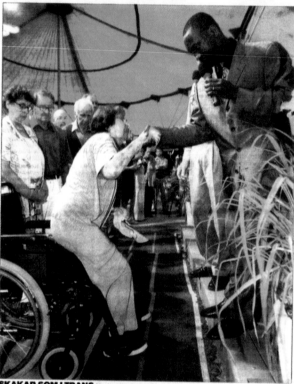

„I have healed people with HIV", says Charles Ndifon in this headline in the Swedish newspaper, Aftonbladet (1 August 2002). In well-organized and disciplined Sweden, where they have laws against all kinds of human behaviour, the head of public prosecution, Sven-Erik Alhems, even tried to prohibit Charles Ndifon from healing...! But after some months he had to concede that there was no case.

# USA: Mind, shut up!

**Rev Anne-Marie Arowora, Santa Rosa Beach, Florida, USA, gives her personal testimony on how she was healed from cancer by the power of the Holy Spirit**

April, 2001

I was diagnosed with metastatic breast cancer that had originated in my left breast and had spread down my backbone down to my lower back.

I was told I had cancer on or about the 2nd of February, 2001. I had called 911 on February 19th as I was unable to get out of bed with excruciating back pain and was taken to three different hospital emergency rooms the three previous days to diagnosis. Finally, my friend threatened to call HRS Abuse Hotline to get me admitted to the Bay Medical center in Panama City, Florida. They ended up giving me all kinds of tests, two or three MRI scans, and two CT scans in which they injected dye into my body. They did a lumpectomy on my left breast, gave me three very strong doses of chemotherapy and fourteen radiation treatments on my back. I stayed in the hospital two and a half weeks and almost three months in a nursing home.

When Pastor Ndifon came to Christian International Church, the church had arranged to transport me from the nursing home and back every evening. I also stayed at home from Thursday until Friday morning. I had received a fourty eight hour leave of absence from the nursing home from the oncologist, but the nursing home social director threatened to kick me out if I left (This was just an attempt from the devil to steal my healing). My response to her was that nobody was going to stop me from going to the miracle crusade. Finally the admissions director came to my aid and they let me go.

I was not strong enough to sit up during the meetings but lay down on the second row of chairs. On Friday 6 April 2001, in the afternoon, I was again in severe pain and cried out for Pastor Ndifon to come and pray for me. He rebuked the pain and the cancer and gave me the best advice of my life. He told me to say "Mind, shut up. Thank you Jesus for my healing." I rested in the Lord in the church the rest of the afternoon and attended the evening meeting. The next day I had to say 'Mind shut up. Thank you Jesus for my healing' every two minutes or so. But I persevered. I also took Pastor's advice about decreasing my morphine and other medications slowly. I also met a lot of resistance when I did this. I remembered that healing is like a seed you plant in the ground: you don't dig up the seed every day, but let it germinate and let it grow up. I also received physical therapy every day to help me walk again. The doctor refused to give me a cancer blood test. He became very angry when I asked him at the end of April or beginning of May. He said that I was not healed. But the last time I saw him two days before I left the nursing home, he did a 180 degree turn and said, "Anne-Marie, you can live a long life. You won't have to die of cancer and the bone pain will go away."

Today, I am off all pain medications, and I'm not taking any morphine (90 mg a day in the beginning). I walk without a walker most of the time and thank the Lord for my healing every day. The devil tried to kill me but Jesus has healed me. I am stronger every day. I prayed for the nurses in the nursing home and the Lord healed them. Christian International Family Church let me give my testimony in church twice about how the Lord healed me.

I am very grateful to Pastor Ndifon for coming to Christian International and praying for me. It saved my life. I might be dead today if he had not come. They expected me to die in the nursing home. The social director always tried to tell me how serious my condition was. But I rebuked her word curses.

Thank you Pastor Charles Ndifon and Donna Ndifon for being obedient to the Lord.

*- Rev. Anne-Marie Arowora,*
*Santa Rosa Beach, Florida*
*(Also published on the website*
*of pastor Charles Ndifon)*

*Arroyo Grande, California*
*- joy after a healing*

# 48 miracles

**More than 500 were healed in Gulf Port, Mississippi. Here is a brief list of 48 miracles reported in just one night...**

When Charles Ndifon and his team had been invited by Pastors Keith and Tanya Thrash of the Pass Road Baptist Church in Gulfport Mississippi, people came from as far as Wisconsin, Maryland, Nebraska, Florida, Oklahoma and Texas. They came to hear and to be healed of their infirmities.

So many Miracles were reported by many even after the meetings were over as over five hundred people were healed by the power of God.

Here is a partial list of Miracles and testimonies from just one night.[1]

As you read, expect a miracle to happen to you today!

**1. One of the ladies** from the church went to a shopping plaza to buy a can of Pepsi for Pastor Charles to drink. There, she met a homeless man who was begging for money. The man was sick and looked hopeless. He asked for some money so he could buy something to eat. This same man had suffered a stroke on his right side that had left him paralyzed and unable to walk.

He confessed later that he had been brought up in a religious environment, which had brought him into a lot of bondage, such as drug, alcohol and nicotine addiction. The lady that he was talking to invited him to come to the Miracle Services that they were having at the church. The man thought to himself, "I did not eat the whole day, I can wait a little longer until the service finishes."

During this time, at the church the service was going on. Pastor Charles had a word of knowledge about people being healed of different sicknesses and one of them was a stroke condition. It was at this time that the man came in with a cane, unable to lift his right hand and leg. As he heard the word and walked down the aisle, he was completely healed. Now he was able to move his hand and leg perfectly. After he was healed the man continued to come the rest of the week at church and was changed. He received Jesus as his

Savior and began to understand his identity.

From being a lonely and homeless man in rags, he was transformed into a prince! By the end of the week he was hardly recognized by the people at the church. He had cut his hair and was well dressed. The Good News is indeed the power!

2. **A little girl around 8 years old** had suffered from a stomach ache for some time. She was perfectly healed during the time that Pastor Charles was ministering to the people.

3. **A young girl** came to the service with a sinus condition that she had had for several years. During the time that Pastor Charles was ministering the power of God touched her and she was completely set free of her sickness.

4. **A lady** came to the meeting suffering from pneumonia and intestinal problems. She had been fighting these conditions for a long time. She was healed completely.

5. **A lady had suffered from stomach discomfort for several years.** During the meeting the discomfort left and she was free.

6. **One of the worship team members** had suffered for several years from chest pain. He came to the meeting believing that he would be healed. The power of God touched him and he was completely set free.

7. **A lady had been suffering from arthritis** in her knees for several years. She came to the church expecting her miracle, and during the service she was completely healed.

8. **A teenager** was having problems with her ankles for several years. They were going down to the ground. During the meeting her ankles were completely straight. She was able to walk with no problems any longer.

9. **A man came to the meeting unable to move his shoulder.** The man was working on a house when he fell down and dislocated his shoulder. He was taken to the emergency room where they put his arm in the right place, but he was still in a lot of pain and at times his arm would become dislocated. He came to the meeting expecting God to touch him. Pastor Charles had a word of knowledge that God wanted to heal someone with a shoulder condition. The man came and was touched by the healing power of God and was able at that moment to move his arm freely with no pain.

10. **A lady that was suffering from lupus and heart problems** came to the meeting knowing that God would heal her. She was not disappointed as she was set free of her sickness.

11. **A teenager** had had problems with her knees popping out for about a

year and a half. She used to play soccer and it was getting really difficult for her to play. She came to the Miracle crusade where she was able to walk and run perfectly! She was healed!!

12. **This lady had suffered** from stomach pain for several years. She was perfectly set free of the discomfort.

13. **One lady had had back surgery** a year ago, which left her in a lot of pain. During the service she felt the pain leave her. She was completely set free!!!!

14. **A lady in her late 50's** had problems with her heart. She had been to the doctors and they could not find what was wrong with her. At the meeting she was healed of her disease.

15. **This lady has had pain** in her legs for several years. While Pastor Charles was sharing, she was completely set free from her pain. She began to walk and the pain was completely gone!!!

16. **A lady suffering with diabetes** for several years came to the meeting expecting God to touch her. She went home and she checked her blood sugar level and it was normal, she was completely healed!!!

17. **An elderly lady had cataracts in her eye** and had suffered from arthritis for several years. She was completely set free of her infirmities. She was able to see and walk normally once again.

18. **A man came to the meeting paralyzed** on his whole left side. He had suffered a stroke some time ago and was unable to move his hand and leg. As he was there, he began to move his right hand for the first time since he had had the stroke. The next day he came to the miracle meeting and Pastor Charles had a word of knowledge that God wanted to heal a person with a left leg condition and he was completely healed. The man began to walk freely without any pain in his body.

19. **A lady in her 40's** came to the meeting with a lot of pain in her legs. After Pastor Charles shared the Word of God, she believed that God could set her free. Pastor Charles commanded the pain to go and she was completely free. She checked the pain and it was gone.

20. **A man came to the meeting with a sciatic nerve pain.** The power of God was present to heal. He was completely set free of his infirmity.

21. **A young lady** came desiring to be able to see perfectly. Her sight was very bad. She believed that God could heal her but she did not know how to receive her healing. Pastor Charles began to teach her. When she arrived home she began to work at the computer and then soon she realized she was

able to see perfectly. She was completely healed!!

22. **Two sisters** came to the miracle meeting with vision impairment. One also had very weak knees. They were completely healed. The one with the knee condition began to walk, perfectly healed.

23. **One lady had been suffering from osteoarthritis** and osteoporosis for 20 years. Her mother suffered from it too, so she was determined that she would receive her freedom that night. After Pastor Charles shared the word of God, she believed and she was completely set free of these infirmities.

24. **One lady in her early 30's suffered with a heart condition** from which she would often pass out. Her mother who believed that God had a destiny for her daughter to fulfill invited her. Pastor Charles also had a word of knowledge that God was going to restore 7 times her dreams. The lady was drastically changed. Her mother had been suffering since 1984 with a collapsed disk and lower back pain. She was completely healed during the time Pastor Charles was ministering to the people. They left together happy, praising the Lord Jesus!!!

25. **One lady in her early 30's had been born with scoliosis.** She came to the meeting with the expectation that she would be healed. Pastor Charles called people with scoliosis saying that God wanted to heal them. She came to the front and Pastor Charles told her to sit on the chair and watch how her leg would grow. She was surprised because she did not know that one of her legs was shorter. She went to different doctors and they could not help her, they could not do anything to make the leg grow. When Pastor Charles commanded the leg to grow, it began to grow. The whole church left praising the Lord for what God was doing. Also her husband had been suffering from intestinal pain and stomach bleeding. He too was completely healed.

26. **One couple** came both suffering from different conditions. The wife had a lump growing on her foot and the husband had been suffering with pain in his back as a result of an accident. The power of God had touched them and both were completely healed. The lump began to shrink and was getting smaller and smaller. The next day they testified that they were completely healed.

27. **One elderly lady was unable to hear out of one ear for 41 years.** This condition was a result of mumps, which she had when she was a few years old. She had also suffered from scoliosis for several years. She believed the word of God and was perfectly set free. She began to hear out of her bad ear, and she was able to walk free of scoliosis.

**28. One lady in her late 40's** had had blurred vision for a long time. When she heard Pastor Charles sharing the Word of God she believed that Jesus could heal her, and her vision was perfectly restored.

**29. A woman in her late 20's** had been suffering for several years with pain in her wrist. She was concerned about it because some of her friends in college had the same condition and they went to the doctor and had to wear a cast on their wrist for life. She believed God could heal her and when Pastor Charles was ministering she believed the word preached and was completely free of that pain. She was able to do things once again with no pain in her wrist.

**30. A man with an asthma** condition that he had suffered from for years came to the meeting tired of that sickness. He had gone to different doctors and had spent a lot of money but they could not help him. During the meeting Pastor Charles gave a word of knowledge concerning people with an asthma condition, that God wanted to set them free. The man believed the word of God and was completely set free of asthma.

**31. A man in his early 30's injured his back.** He was moving an entertainment system weighing around 250 kg, and he pulled a muscle. He went to the doctors and received a lot of medicine but the pain was still there. As Pastor Charles was ministering the power of God was present to heal and the man's back was completely restored.

**32. Another man** in his late 30's suffered with back problems. He had been healed several months ago, but did not know how to keep his healing. Because of the morning teachings he was able to apply what Pastor Charles taught and was completely healed.

**33. A lady came to the meeting expecting** that God would meet all her needs. She had written down a big list. She and her husband were not able to have children, she had vision problems, and she also had a lump on her breast. During the time Pastor Charles was ministering to the people she began to check herself. The lump was gone and she was able to see perfectly!!!

**34. One night**, while Pastor Charles had been calling out different sicknesses that God wanted to heal, he called out cancer. A man in his early 30's walked down the aisle and Pastor Charles told him to go show himself to the doctor because God had set him free. Several days later he came back with a report from the doctor that where once there was cancer there now was scar tissue. The man was completely restored!

**35. A Mexican man** had had osteoarthritis for twenty years and came to the meeting in a lot of pain. The arthritis had spread all over his body. He also had been suffering with dry eyes and kidney problems. During the meeting, he was completely healed of all his conditions.

36. An elderly lady was suffering from diabetes and mental problems. She believed God's word and was completely healed and restored.

37. A lady with fibril tumors came to the miracle meeting. Also six months ago she had been diagnosed with hypertension. She had been addicted to nicotine. The power of God touched her and she was completely set free and delivered.

38. One lady had had blood clots for 5 years and had suffered from migraines for a long time. She also had varicose veins on her leg and was afraid to go to the doctor again to have her leg checked. She had been struggling with fear all her life. Pastor Charles bean to minister the Gospel to her. She believed the Word of God and she was completely set free!!

39. A young boy around 8 years old came to the miracle crusade, unable to speak. Pastor Charles commanded the mute spirit to go. When he was asked to say his name, the boy began to speak perfectly. Since than he has been able to speak perfectly. **His mother** who was a believer brought the boy to the meeting. Later on she confessed that she had had two lumps on her body for several years. One on the left side of her head and one on her side. As Pastor Charles and Donna Ndifon were ministering to them the power of God touched her and the lumps began to shrink down.

40. A young lady had lower back pain, which had caused numbness in her leg for several years. The power of God touched her and she was completely restored.

41. A young man came with intestinal problems caused by a colitis surgery that he had had several years ago. He had also had an accident 3 years ago which left him with a knot in his shoulder. During the time Pastor Charles was ministering, the man was completely healed.

42. A 4-year-old girl was brought to the miracle crusade with an asthma condition. During the meeting she was completely set free.

43. A lady in her early 30's had been suffering from depression for a while. Because of her condition she was having chest pain which led her to go to different doctors. The doctors could not do anything for her. As she was coming daily to the meetings, she was healed.

44. A lady was brought to the meeting in a wheelchair because of liver cancer. One of her kidneys had been taken out because the cancer was

spreading all over her body. The lady, believing the Word preached, stood up and began to walk around. She had no more pain in her body and she began to feel strength coming back to her.

**45. An elderly lady crippled from polio** when she was 2 years old began to walk perfectly straight. She was completely healed!!

**46. A lady in her early 30's was born with a gland disease.** She was completely healed. She began to move her neck and there was no more pain. She was completely free!

**47. A woman had been suffering with cataracts** in her left eye. She was supposed to have surgery on that eye the week of the miracle services, but the doctor called and postponed the surgery for the coming week which gave her a chance to come to the miracle meetings and be healed. She believed the Word that Pastor Charles was teaching and she was completely healed of her condition.

**48. A lady in her late 40's** had been suffering from arthritis for several years. She came to the meeting in a lot of pain. During the time of ministry to the sick, the power of God touched her and she was completely healed.

## Healed from Coma

When Charles Ndifon was preaching at Sierra Faith Center, Mariposa, California, a lady opened her eyes from coma. Cecil Howard reports:[2]

"We just received a phone call from a pastor of one of the largest churches in Fresno. He personally received a miracle healing in his foot and ankle during our Friday night healing service.

It was also during that service that he asked for prayer for his sister-in-law in Colorado. She and her husband pastor an Assembly of God church in Colorado. She had been in a coma since brain surgery for a cerebral hemorrhage last week. The doctors did not expect her to live.

As Charles prayed, He called her life back to her and commanded her consciousness to return. He then said go call your family and check it out, she is going to be all right!

Well, the good news is ... she opened her eyes Sunday morning and recognized her family! The family now believes for a full and complete recovery."

After gradually becoming blind and deaf, this woman was totally healed at the Miracle meetings. See how her expression changed!

# India: Children healed

**50,000 received Jesus in India during one month of meetings in Kerala, Tamil Nadu and Goa state.**

In 2000, Charles Ndifon was in India, together with a team made up of Dan McLean and Richard Smith. Over one month, thousands were helped with their illnesses, and according to statements from the organizers, over fifty thousand Indians publicly declared that they wanted Jesus to be Lord in their lives. Assistance was given by local pastor Y.S. Deva Sunderam and his team in Tamil Nadu and pastors Victor and Julie Affonso and team in Goa.

There are always big numbers reported when Charles Ndifon travels in Africa or Asia. Perhaps the big response is due to the fact that people don't have as many theological reservations as we do in the West, but pay more attention to whether there is power behind the words. And there is, when Charles Ndifon preaches.

Realistically, one has to question whether the fifty thousand Indians who testified that they want to believe in Jesus actually will become Christians in practice. For Hindus, it's no big problem to accept Jesus as one more god among the many others they already worship. It's often said that there are just as many gods in Hinduism as there are Hindus, because each person can just make their own god. But according to the Bible, those kind of self-made "gods" are only idols. They are an expression of superstition. But in this spiritual openness, it is easy for all kinds of spirits to gain power over people. And it's only when one has to choose between the spirits that it becomes apparent whether Jesus has become Lord in one's life. Therefore, belief in the Almighty God requires one to drop these self-made gods:

"Then you will defile your idols overlaid with silver and your images covered with gold; you will throw them away like a menstrual cloth and say to them, 'Away with you!'" (Isaiah 30:22).

After the fifty thousand had experienced the Spirit's power and had received this power from Jesus in their lives, it was easier for them to part with these "mute idols".

## Kerala, Tamil Nadu

The healing meetings in India were held in four towns. In three of the towns, local believers were trained in continuing the work of preaching the gospel and healing in Jesus' name.

The first week was spent in Anapara in Kerela State with thousands in attendance. Great miracles took place as the Gospel was proclaimed. About seven thousand five hundred decided to follow Jesus after having seen the many healings which happened.

The second week Pastor Charles and his team preached in the town of Karungal, in the state of Tamil Nadu, where the crowd numbered over seven thousand to twenty five thousand per night. Here, over two nights, over ten thousand were reported to have accepted Jesus Christ as Lord on each night! Great miracles confirmed the Gospel preached.

## The rain stopped...

The third week, Pastor Charles and his team ministered in the city of Nagercoil, also in Tamil Nadu. One of the most outstanding miracles was the *"miracle of the rain"*. Pastor Charles prayed and the rain stopped for five days during the crusade in the middle of the monsoon. It rained everywhere in Nagercoil except on the crusade ground.

The fourth week, they ministered in the State of Goa. More healing miracles were documented here than anywhere else during this month.

Here there also was the miracle of the rain, and fourty deaf mutes were healed among other extraordinary miracles. And people were set free from oppressive spirits.

## Miracle at the hospital

A great miracle took place at the Goa University Medical Center. Between thirty five to fourty children were healed and discharged after the power of God healed them when Charles Ndifon prayed for them. As the Bible declares "Jesus laid hands on each one of them and healed them all".

The children were suffering from various sicknesses and diseases, such as aids, tumors, cancers, diabetes, some were even in comas. They were all healed by the power of God!

From India, Abigail Fernandes sent these pictures and this letter:

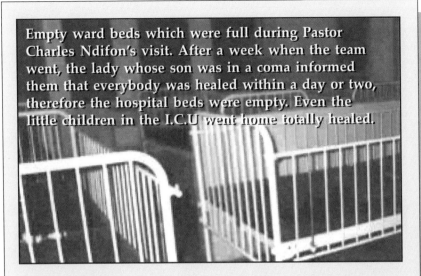

Empty ward beds which were full during Pastor Charles Ndifon's visit. After a week when the team went, the lady whose son was in a coma informed them that everybody was healed within a day or two, therefore the hospital beds were empty. Even the little children in the I.C.U went home totally healed.

*Dear Charles,*

Hi! I am really excited about what the Lord is doing in Goa.

Sorry about not sending in my testimony the day I promised to, because I wanted to also send in the latest report from the hospital ministry after you left India.

Yesterday, the 7th September 2000, I visited the hospital, ie. the Childrens ward you had ministered in and guess what? THE WARD THAT WAS FULL IS NOW EMPTY AND ALL THE CHILDREN AND THE MOTHERS YOU PRAYED FOR WERE DISCHARGED IN A DAY OR TWO.

Not only that, the baby who had AIDS went home totally healed.

There was a boy about 12-13 years old who was in a coma (and the doctors had given up) and you prayed with him too. Now he is

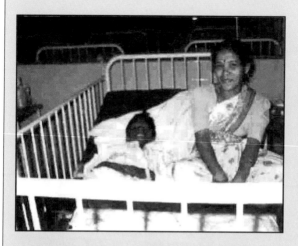

out of coma, totally cured and can eat and drink everything and runs about and plays like a normal child. His mother was so overjoyed. I have taken pictures of him and his mother and the empty ward too.

The boy who had drunk kerosene is now healed and is totally healthy. I thank the Lord, Charles, for bringing you to India and touching the lives of thousands of sick and hopeless people.

May the Lord Jesus bless you, your wife and your sons in a mighty way. - *Abigail Fernandes*

(Photographs and text by Abigail Fernandez, Goa, India, used by permission of Christlove Ministries.)

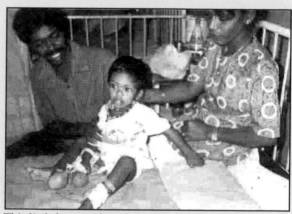

*This little boy accidentally drank kerosene and was dying, he was unconscious. He was in a glass cubicle with oxygen going through, but within a week after Charles prayed the boy revived and was well enough to leave the hospital.*

# Mexico: Look!

## The Anatomy of two Miracles in Mexico City, Mexico
## April, 1999

This gentleman came to the miracle crusade with his family and his doctor to hear and to be healed by Jesus Christ.

He had been diagnosed with terminal cancer which had affected his whole body and had left him completely immobile, paralyzed, and in a lot of pain. He had been given up by the doctors and had been told to go home and get his affairs in order. With no hope, he heard of all that Jesus had been doing at the crusade. How the blind saw, the deaf heard, and the crippled walked as Jesus Christ touched them with his love.

Rev Charles Ndifon preached to the crowd of over ten thousand that had gathered on this night, that the power of the Lord was present to heal them. Thousands responded when they were asked to receive Jesus Christ as their Lord and savior. After the prayer for salvation, Pastor Charles Ndifon called for those with incurable and

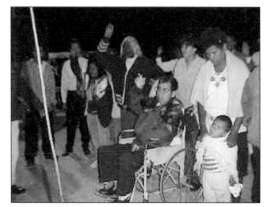

*He listens as Rev. Charles Ndifon teaches about Jesus Christ.*

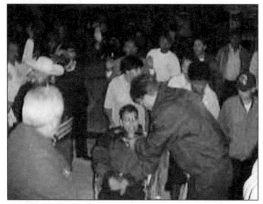

*Pastor Roberto Stevenson translates as pastor Charles interviews him about His condition just minutes before his miracle!*

terminal sicknesses to come to the front for a demonstration that Jesus can

111

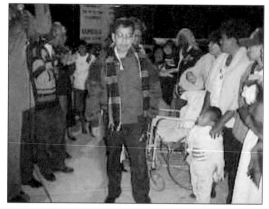

heal even terminal cases. That there was no sickness that was incurable, no case too hard for Jesus to heal.

The gentleman was one of the thousands that was healed that night! He was wheeled forward in his wheelchair. Though He had been given up by the doctors, he came expecting a miracle from God!

*Pastor Charles (in a grey suit on the left) commanded him to stand up and walk in Jesus' name! He arose and walked, and he made the discovery that every pain and paralysis had left him. He began to praise the Lord for the wonders of what He had done for him.*

*After walking around the crusade grounds without any aid, strength returned to his whole body. He then proceeded to push his wheelchair as his doctor (in yellow with a dark neck-tie) all smiles, looks on rejoicing with him!*

*He pushed his wheelchair home praising God and waving as the multitude rejoiced and applauded, glorifying Jesus Christ.*

## New lungs...?

Rev. Charles Ndifon noticed this dear woman when he arrived on the crusade grounds. She was carried to the crusade by her family on a stretcher, the same way several hundred others were carried also.

Some were carried in wheelbarrows, rolled-up in mats or their lifeless bodies were wrapped in blankets and clothing. They came from all the surrounding cities and regions to Mexico City to hear the good news of Jesus Christ and to be healed by him of all manner of sicknesses and various diseases.

*The lady (lying down) and someone making her as comfortable as possible.*

When Rev. Charles came to them, he encouraged them to "fear not" and only believe!

As Rev. Charles was preaching that the power of the Lord was present to heal the people. The power of the Lord began to heal her as she was carried from the stretcher to a wheelchair. Her lungs had been removed she could not breath without the cylinder attached to her and she was awaiting her death.

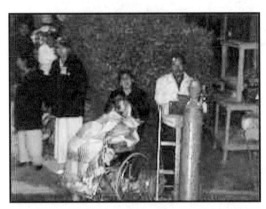

*To her left is a giant oxygen tank which she was connected to. Her lungs had been removed.*

The doctors had done their best, but they could not help her.

After thousands had responded to the Gospel, it was now time to display the power of God again. This night, the example miracle prayer before the masses was for those with missing body parts (Matthew 15:30). The lady came forward to receive new lungs. Others with missing eardrums, hips, kidneys etc.

Pastor Aurellio did the interview about her condition. She went on to describe her condition, how the doctors had given her up and she had been confined to bed for years, awaiting death..

113

Charles Ndifon approaches her to tell her that her case is not impossible. He commanded new lungs to be formed in her, and the oxygen cylinder was removed. Immediately, she started breathing freely!
Charles Ndifon puts out his hand and commands her to rise up and walk in the name of Jesus Christ!

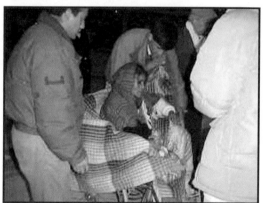

She throws open her blanket that was used to wrap her on the stretcher. With a little help to steady her, she stands up and begins to walk!

As she kept walking her strength returned completely. She was exercising herself for the first time in years without the aid of the oxygen tanks. The Woman walks home without her tank to the amazement of the crowd, as they glorified Jesus Christ. At that same time, thousands of Miracles started taking place all over the crusade ground.

# Hindu Doctor
# Healed of Epilepsy

**„I saw wonderful, indisputable miracles."**

"I was born in India, but when I was seven years old, my family moved to Denmark", explains Dr. Alok Shukla, who holds a Ph. D. in Molecular Biology.

"I've been living in Denmark for the last twent years, and I also did my schooling here. Even though my family practices Hinduism, I've always been an atheist.

After finishing my PhD in August last year (1999) I was planning to travel to India to get a treatment for my epilepsy before starting working. I've actually had epilepsy for ten years, and I was on medication continuously during that time. At one time the doctor cut the medication for one day to half dosage. I was immediately overcome with seizures. I was, of course put back on full medication right away.

When Charles Ndifon was in Denmark, I went to his meetings. I saw wonderful things and received prayer for healing.

The result? I was totally healed. I now take no medication. It is so good to be free. Still, I was faced with a dilemma. Until that time I was an atheist but I was forced, because of the miracle, to investigate the claims of Christ on my life and to begin reading the Bible.

One month later Bob Brasset was in Denmark. Again I saw wonderful, indisputable miracles. Convinced that Jesus is the Son of God this time, I committed my heart to Christ.

I was born again and heard the voice of the Holy Spirit telling me to be baptized in water. I obeyed and got an added bonus! Jesus came along and baptized me in the Holy Spirit too! I prayed in a brand new prayer language I didn't ever learn. (Although I speak in several natural languages.)

Then Jesus began healing the sick through me. Jesus is so wonderful. I am filled with love and glorious freedom.

I will never be the same. Thank you Jesus!"

**West Kootenay trails**
page 12

# Weekly

*Missing husb...*
**Ask Wend...**
page 12

*Vol. 6 No. 37* · **Wednesday September 16, 1998** · *Every Wednesday — Every Home*

# Faith Healing

**Over one thousand people flocked to Cranbrook last week to hear the message that evangelist Charles Ndifon was preaching — and, God willing, to witness a miracle.**

**By Christine Boyd**
**Weekly Editor**

The miracle felt like a soft

to take any of her regular dosage of pills since that day, she said, nor has she had any recurrence of arthritic pain.

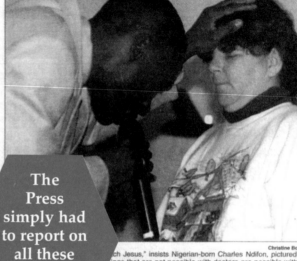

*Christine Boy...*

...ch Jesus," insists Nigerian-born Charles Ndifon, pictured a...
...ings that are not possible with doctors are possible with G...

▼ Back page                    ▶ Page 5

## Daily News
*The Virgin Islands*

*A Pulitzer Prize-winning newspaper*

# Faith and Values

*Saturday, July 3, 1999 ▼ Page 38*

▼ Inside
Pastor Abukua Todi
on the family

## God's healing powe...

### Evangelist holds healing services at VI Christian Mini...

# the power to heal

NEW LONDON COUNTY · WINDHAM COUNTY

## Eastern Connecticut

# Today

...day @ Bulletin
...VEMBER 18, 1997

**Nancy Hall**
*StreetSeen*

# ...ealer ...rings ...iracles ...city

# Canada: Documented Healing

**June Hunter who was healed from cancer tells her story in this interview from a Canadian newspaper**

## Cancer survivor says faith healer saved her

- *Do you believe in miracles?* June Hunter does.

Three months ago Hunter was dying and there was no remedy for the cancer that was killing her. Today, she's cured.

Hunter's miracle came after she exhausted the remedies held out by modern medicine to rid her body of intermediate grade lymphoma.

Last year, the Sooke school district employee's waning strength and general fatigue precipitated a six month leave of absence from her job.

That was the beginning of the downward spiral which lead to Hunter's eventual diagnosis of non-Hodgkins Lymphoma, the most difficult of the lymphomas to deal with, according to Hunter.

"It's fast growing. It spread through my body in about six weeks. I looked about five-months pregnant. I was so bloated with retained lymphatic fluid."

*Dr Nicol MacPherson*, oncologist with the *Victoria Cancer Treatment Center* prescribed multiagent chemotherapy to treat the cancer which had spread to Hunter's chest, abdomen and peripheral (neck, armpits and groin) nodes.

At the end of the five-month treatment course Dr. MacPherson showed "an apparent complete response." But the disease raced back within a few weeks. "I caved in. I was terrified," Hunter said.

As a last resort, Hunter traveled to Vancouver in hopes of obtaining a bone marrow transplant. On the basis of her medical charts and her prognosis, she was rejected as a candidate for treatment and advised that she should spend the few weeks she had left to live with her family.

When the Hunters pushed for a reversal of the decision, they were informed she had less than a ten per cent chance of surviving, even after the transplant.

"This was a real blow as you can imagine," Hunter said.

But she had no intention of dying.

"I have three daughters sixteen, nineteen and twenty one and I was not going to inflict that grief on them."

It was then that Hunter began praying for a miracle.

"I knew God had a plan."

Back in Victoria MacPherson started Hunter on a dose of palliative chemotherapy which was intended simply to shrink the disease to extend what little life she had left.

"We knew we could no longer exert a cure," Dr. MacPherson said.

In February, Hunter's pastor came to her with an invitation to accompany a pastoral team from the Trinity Christian Center to a conference on Christ's Healing Miracles in Connecticut. That was where she met evangelist Charles Ndifon. It was there that her life was renewed.

"The first day Charles knelt down, looked me in the eyes and said, 'the Lord told me before the service that as you listened to the Gospel the cancer would die.'"

Hunter says the revelation that she was really healed took place after the second or third session of the conference.

Her healing has been documented by her oncologist.

"Since her faith healing, the disease has shrunk and the only palpable lymph node is in her axilla," Dr. MacPherson said.

"This is dramatic since Hunter had disease race back within a few weeks of completing high-dose chemotherapy and yet she has been off all chemo since January."

Dr. MacPherson is cautious when speaking about cures—not just when alternative treatments are given but also with conventional chemo and radiation. „We need to wait for years to say that. However we can say that her good health now is a pleasant surprise."

Hunter believes God brought her life—a life that until recently was painfully slipping away from her.

"I can't tell enough people," Hunter said, "You read about this kind of thing in Reader's Digest and it's always about someone in Illinois or somewhere like that."

Article written by Ginny McInnes, published June 1998, used with kind permission from Sooky News Mirror, Vancouver Is., Canada.

# England: Miracle Man

**Journalists are often in a dilemma when they have to report on miracles. They are trained to be skeptical and they know "it can't be" – but here they see it...**

## MIRACLE MAN
### (from Scarborough Evening News)

"WORSHIPPERS at Scarborough Christian Fellowship have been stunned by a series of apparent miracles performed by a healer from Nigeria. Charles Ndifon has amazed the congregation at the church in Castle Road by appearing to cure various ailments before their eyes.

The Nigerian, who is based in the United States, travels the world performing his feats.

During the meetings in Scarborough this week several worshippers say they have been cured of all aches, pains and serious medical problems that have troubled them for years.

Mr. Ndifon said: Right here in Scarborough many people have been healed already. I have a written testimony from one, Edwin Jeffery, a man with arthritis who could hardly walk.

Last night after his healing he was dancing and amazed that his pain had totally gone.

There may be people in this community who are sick and don't

HEALED ... Edwin Jeffery, left, does a jig after having his arthritic knees cured and Tracey Pashby is all smiles after faith healer Charles Ndifon eased her bad back.

know about this. They have nothing to lose by coming along. It's totally free.

This week a Scarborough man who had one leg half an inch shorter than the other since suffering a childhood illness said his leg was noticeably longer after the healing session.

Philip Coles, 34, of Westwood Gardens, said: "I developed the condition when I was six. I could not walk for two and a half years until I completed medical treatment but even then I still had poor mobility.

I was in the meeting when God told Charles that someone in the room had a problem with their leg. I came forward because I was the only one there with that problem.

He prayed for me and after a few minutes I felt a difference in my leg. I believe that it is longer than it was but I've yet to get it checked by a doctor. Another member of the fellowship, Tracey Pashby, 37, of Barwick Street, had a back problem cured. She said: I've had a bad back since Christmas, when I tore a muscle. It s been stiff and sore all the time. Charles didn't actually pray for me but while I was in the meeting I felt something change in my back. Since I hurt my back I haven t been able to touch my head on my knees, something I could do all my life. When I felt the change I ran in the other room to see if I could do it and I can.

I went up to the front of the room to tell everyone about it. I can t describe the feeling I had. It was amazing.

Mr. Ndifon was born in Nigeria. He was in his fifth year of mechanical engineering studies when he discovered his gift.

He said: Jesus appeared to me. Shortly after that I was visiting the terminal ward of a hospital and all the patients were miraculously healed.

This year he has visited fourteen countries and his campaign will take him to India, Sri Lanka, Russia and Norway.

Dr Phil Garnett, a GP in Filey, said people should be wary. If people wish to try an alternative therapy of any kind then that is their decision, he said. I would advise them to be careful that people who claim to have the power to heal are genuine, particularly if money is involved. Anyone with health problems must seek standard medical attention.

*(End of article by Lauren Hopkins from Scarborough Evening News 24.2.2000, used with permission.)*

# The Philippines: Blind man's pupils restored

## It happened out on the street!

When Pastor Charles Ndifon was in the Philippines from 26 March to 2 April 2002, as usual, a lot of miracles took place in Jesus' name. The campaign was held in Dipolog City and Cagayan de Oro City. But there was one miracle which was quite exceptional – and it happened out on the street!

One day Charles took a relaxed walk around the town in which the campaign was being held. He was wearing shorts, a trendy cap on his head – with the brim backwards – and smart black and white shoes. All right!

Beside the road sat a young man in the shade under some palm trees, playing the banjo to earn his keep. The man was blind, it turned out. In front of him stood a plastic container, into which passers by threw coins to help him. Behind him sat an elderly lady. She may have been his mother.

"I thought: 'Now it's time to have some fun on the street', says Charles." And by 'fun on the street', Charles means God's power in action among ordinary people.

"I went over to him and told him about Jesus, who heals the sick. I asked him if he wanted to be able to see, and he said yes. Of course he would like to see. But when I looked into his eyes I noticed that the man's pupil was completely covered with a white film in his left eye. Wow! This called for a

121

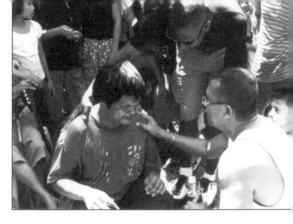

real miracle. So I began to pray for him. I commanded his eyes to be healed in Jesus' name. I commanded his eyes to receive pupils", says Charles, as we look through his photographs in his room late one night after the campaign in Kolding a few months later that same year.

"So the man is sitting there with his banjo, while I stand there praying. And eventually a small crowd gathered around us", says Charles. "They wanted to see what was going on. And God did big things that day! Man, I tell you! As we watched – as we stood there on the street looking at the man, a small black dot gradually grew in his eye, and eventually it got bigger, and in the end there was a pupil, and the man began to see!"

"God is great! Look here", says Charles, and shows me the pictures.

"Look at this: Here his eye is still white, the man can't see anything, there's no visible pupil. Here something has begun to appear… And here there is a whole and perfect pupil…

It was wonderful to see it happen."

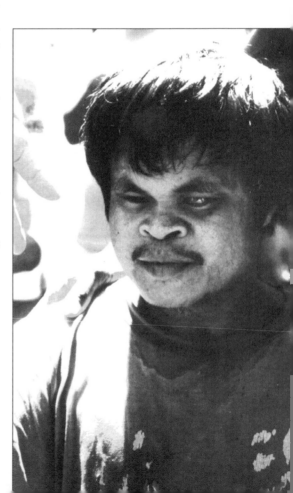

*The man on the street with no visible pupil has now got a pupil in his left eye and he begins to see.*

# Part 2
# Follow up

# Who is this Charles Ndifon?

**Who is this Charles Ndifon, who is now healing the sick by the thousands – apparently with no regard for how serious their illnesses are?**

He was born in 1969 and is therefore only in his early thirties.

"But I'm older than Jesus was when he appeared in public", Ndifon notes with an ironic smile, because some critics among Christian leaders in the USA have hinted that he is too *young* to do what he is doing. They think he should submit to older and more experienced leaders. But Charles is not impressed by American or European church life.

"There are too many opinions and too little obedience to what Jesus says we should do. The problem with the West is that you are too comfortable..."

## Little brother with 13 siblings

Charles is the youngest of fourteen children. His family lived in a small town, Ikom, in Cross River State in southern Nigeria. It is situated just 10 km from the border with Cameroon. It is in the tropical, very fertile part of Africa where the rainy season is long and the humidity is high. The temperature is mostly above thirty degrees centigrade. Bananas grow here in enormous bunches, and coffee and cocoa are exported. Millions of liters of palm oil are tapped from vast plantations. Even so, the local population are still often poor. Most of the money rarely goes to the local workers.

"The town I come from is so small that you would have trouble finding it on a map of the country, but God saw me and knew my heart. He knew I would be obedient. And he used me to speak to hundreds of thousands of people", says Charles, full of wonder over the fact that God didn't choose any of the well-known "big names" to perform so many great healings.

"I once had a dream that I was going to become the father of children with many different types of ethnic backgrounds. But in my ignorance I perverted

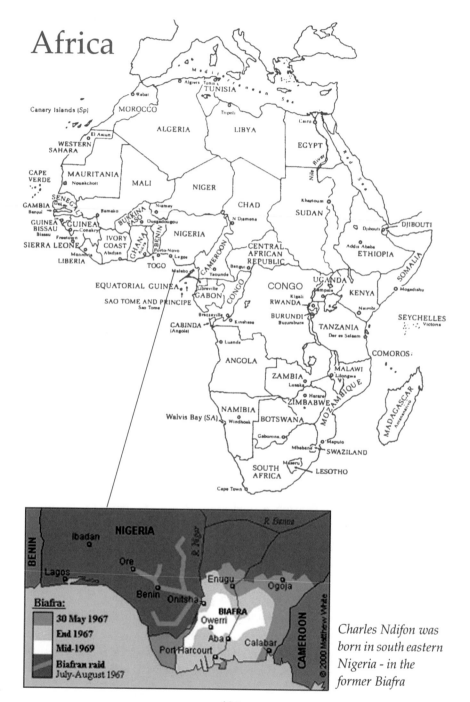

# Africa

Canary Islands (Sp)

MOROCCO

TUNISIA

ALGERIA

LIBYA

EGYPT

WESTERN
SAHARA

El Aaiun

CAPE
VERDE

MAURITANIA

Nouakchott

MALI

NIGER

CHAD

SUDAN

Khartoum

DJIBOUTI

Djibouti

GAMBIA

Banjul

SENEGAL

Dakar

Bamako

Niamey

GUINEA
BISSAU

Bissau

GUINEA

Conakry

Freetown

BURKINA
FASO

Ouagadougou

N Djamena

Addis Ababa

ETHIOPIA

SIERRA LEONE

Monrovia

IVORY
COAST

Abidjan

GHANA

Accra

BENIN

NIGERIA

Porto-Novo

Lagos

CENTRAL
AFRICAN
REPUBLIC

Bangui

SOMALIA

Mogadishu

LIBERIA

TOGO

Malabo

Yaounde

CAMEROON

CONGO

UGANDA

Kampala

KENYA

Nairobi

EQUATORIAL GUINEA

Libreville

GABON

CONGO

Kigali

RWANDA

BURUNDI

Bujumbura

SEYCHELLES

Victoria

SAO TOME AND PRINCIPE

Sao Tome

Brazzaville

Kinshasa

TANZANIA

Dar es Salaam

CABINDA
(Angola)

Luanda

COMOROS

ANGOLA

ZAMBIA

Lusaka

MALAWI

Lilongwe

MADAGASCAR

Antananarivo

NAMIBIA

Walvis Bay (SA)

Windhoek

ZIMBABWE

Harare

MOZAMBIQUE

BOTSWANA

Gaborone

Maputo

Mbabane

SWAZILAND

SOUTH
AFRICA

Maseru

LESOTHO

Cape Town

---

Biafra:

- 30 May 1967
- End 1967
- Mid-1969
- Biafran raid
July-August 1967

NIGERIA

Ibadan

BENIN

Lagos

Ore

R. Niger

R. Benue

Benin

Onitsha

Enugu

Ogoja

BIAFRA

Owerri

Aba

Calabar

Port Harcourt

CAMEROON

© 2000 Matthew White

*Charles Ndifon was
born in south eastern
Nigeria - in the
former Biafra*

126

this vision from God in my heart. I imagined that I was going to have many wives, as we often have in Africa. I was going to have one black, one white, one Asian, one Indian and many other wives. And I myself thought it was a brilliant idea", Charles laughs.

"Later I understood that the vision was about the 'spiritual children' I was going to have. That is, people who come to faith because I told them the gospel."

## Grew up during the Biafran war

Charles' hometown belonged to the Eastern Nigeria region, which attempted on May 30, 1967 to break away under the leadership of Colonel Ojukwu as an independent republic, Biafra, with over twelve million residents – particularly Christians from the Ibo tribe. They wouldn't accept being ruled over by the country's Muslim majority in the North.

It was in the south-eastern part of the country that all the oil reserves lay, and it was here that industrial development had come the furthest. Charles Ndifon himself belongs

Nigerian soldiers in Biafra 1970

to a very small tribe, which basically only exists in the town of Ikom. He explains:

"We often say that in the south east, with us, is all the money, the south west has the bureaucrats and the north has all the politicians."

The capital, Lagos, was located in the south western part of the country, containing all the government institutions. (In 1983, the capital was moved to Abuja in the middle of the country). In the north – where there was the least development – lived the Muslim half of the population which has always held on solidly to power, not least after the civil war over Biafra which followed the secession. Naturally the rest of Nigeria didn't want to lose the country's 'bread basket'. Two million people – predominantly Ibo tribesman in the North – died in the bloody civil war, before the Nigerian army under General Gowon succeeded in subduing Biafra on January 12th 1970.

## Jesus Christ Airline

For many older people, the Biafran war has special significance. Through the church emergency aid organizations, they were involved in saving Biafra's population from the starvation caused by the Nigerian blockade.

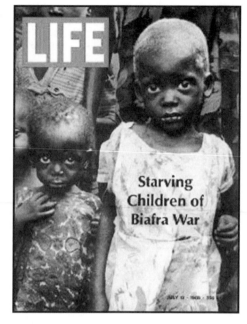

An air bridge was established from the Fernando Po Island in the Gulf of Guinea, using a team of death-defying pilots who flew in the aid. (One of the pilots, Count Carl Gustav von Rosen, Sweden, even took part directly in the war using small, light, MFI-9 private planes armed with rockets. He was later murdered in Ethiopia).

The air bridge was given the name JCA, Joint Christian Aid – but in everyday language pilots and journalists called the enterprise "Jesus Christ Airlines". One of the journalists, Frederick Forsyth, got his big breakthrough with his debut book, "The Biafra Story" (1969) and become a world-famous author.

In an extensive BBC documentary about JCA it was estimated that about 1 million people were actually saved by the air bridge. The program was produced by journalist Lasse Jensen, who himself worked with refugees in Biafra, before later becoming a correspondent in Washington.

## His father was unjustly arrested

Charles Ndifon was only two years old when the civil war broke out, and four when it ended. For Charles and his family the civil war had an unpleasant side effect. Charles' father was one of the leaders in the town, and was employed as a civil servant by the Nigerian government. He was therefore arrested in confusion by the new Biafran authorities.

He wasn't on "the wrong side" in any way, but he had some enemies who used the opportunity to have him removed when the civil war broke out. Later, when the war was over, he was driven back to the village in a motorcade and received with great honor by the whole town.

Charles remembers that his father had a long beard, but was otherwise a complete stranger to the little boy, who hadn't seen him during the first important years of his life.

## Grew up with the Catholic church

Charles grew up with the Roman Catholic church to which his family belonged.

"My family were very devout and we always went to church. We attended mass six days a week – at five in the morning. Apart from Sunday when there was high mass, and when we also went to church.

On many occasions I have almost fallen asleep as I knelt and prayed and my older brothers and sisters gave me a nudge", Charles recalls. Despite everything he had a positive impression of the church.

"Yes, I actually wanted to be a priest – but in reality, God was a complete mystery to me, and I had no personal relationship to Jesus. It wasn't until university that I discovered that was possible", explains Charles Ndifon.

## Very ambitious tribe

"After basic school, I began instead to train as a machine engineer at the University of Nigeria. We have always been very ambitious in our family, in fact in my whole tribe people are very industrious.

The church has also had a big influence here. My father has also contributed a lot to the development of our town. We also stick together in our tribe and town; we encourage and help each other to fight against poverty and to achieve as much as possible.

For example, many of my brothers have PhD's. I myself had the ambition of doing my PhD before I turned 21. That would have allowed me to overtake all my thirteen siblings!", laughs Charles. Charles absolutely doesn't fit with the stereotype image of the very relaxed, laid back African. (The author has lived in Africa for three years and written many articles and a whole book about these relaxed, "typical Africans" – but Charles Ndifon completely breaks this image. He's a dynamo of God's grace!)

## Christianity without power – and with it...!

"I still went to church faithfully, but the Christians I knew didn't make sense to me; I couldn't recognize the Christianity which is talked about in the New Testament in them, neither in myself nor in my surroundings. I was spiritually empty inside."

"That was Christian *tradition* without power", he says.

"People talked a lot about the fact that Jesus was now in heaven, and eternal life, but nothing about what Christianity meant for us here and now. I knew the Bible, but only as literature. I knew what was written in it, but it wasn't until I went to University and met other Christians that I understood what power there is in that book.

These were Bible-believing Christians who didn't only read what it said, as if it was just history, but who lived it and experienced that it was reliable.

These Christians were full of life and showed genuine love to their fellow human beings. This was how I discovered that Christianity was much more than just 'religion'".

## What does it mean to be born again?

Charles Ndifon says that it was then that he was "born again".

The expression comes from the account in the New Testament where Jesus talks to Nicodemus, the Jewish religious leader, during the night (because Nicodemus didn't dare to come during the day when everyone could see him). The wise Nicodemus wanted to understand the new theology Jesus was preaching, but Jesus cut through the theological and philosophical speculation and told him straight out, "no one can see the kingdom of God unless he is born again." (John 3:3)

*"What does it mean to be born again?"*

Jesus gives the astonished Nicodemus a somewhat cryptic answer:

"no one can enter the kingdom of God unless he is born of water and the Spirit. Flesh gives birth to flesh, but the Spirit gives birth to spirit. You should not be surprised at my saying, 'You must be born again.'

The wind blows wherever it pleases. You hear its sound, but you cannot tell where it comes from or where it is going. So it is with everyone born of the Spirit." (John 3:5-8)

## When faith becomes living

To be born again is "to begin all over again". It is to be filled by the Holy

Spirit so that Christianity becomes alive to you and you begin to understand what you didn't understand before. And Jesus is no longer just a historical figure or an exalted mystical deity, but a living reality in your life – as if he lived among us today and was a good friend.

Millions of Christians have had this "born again" experience – either when they began to believe, or at some later time when their faith became living – and they could understand what had been dim before.

(However, some people call themselves born-again Christians out of tradition, without necessarily being so. Just as some Christians think they are "converted" or reformed because they belong to a Christian movement which uses that expression, even though they haven't remotely turned from anything, but live as they always have done).

To be born again also means to "bury your old self" – and surrender your life to God.

## Hard decision to have blind faith

For Charles Ndifon it wasn't easy at all to make that decision:

"I was studying to be an engineer at the University of Nigeria, and I had absolutely no desire to believe blindly in Jesus. I had always imagined that you had to be very desperate before you surrendered your life to God. But suddenly I saw all around me that it was all the clever and capable people who were being born again.

That helped me.

At that time my brother died. He had begun to mix with protestant Christians. Therefore, the Catholic church to which we had always belonged wouldn't give him a Christian burial, since he no longer was a practicing Catholic. As if it meant anything to him where he was buried! When I die, you can do what you like with my body", says Charles.

"For my brother it was unimportant, he was dead and happy with God, but for the rest of the family it was hard. I don't think it was right for the church to have acted in that way. It got me to break out of my old religious ways of thinking and to listen to other Christians.

One of my new Christian friends told me how I could receive Jesus in my heart and have a personal relationship with him.

I knelt down, and for the first time I prayed a personal, and not just liturgical, prayer to God. It changed my life – from that day on my daily life was never the same again.

## Teenager heals the sick

When Charles surrendered his life to God, he meant it seriously. He began to consistently *believe and live according to* what is written in the New Testament – without theological reservations of any kind:

"A lot of theology is just excuses for not doing what we well know we should do", he says.

"I would rather have the 'real thing' – the Bible itself. Why take an indirect route?"

Together with the other young Christians at the university, Charles experienced fantastic miracles when they told others of their faith and when they prayed for the sick – which is quite normal among Christians in Africa. Many go on campaigns in non-Christian villages where they are often confronted with occult spiritual powers and demons. They take part enthusiastically in campaigns, and most are active in choirs, women's associations, the church's social work, student work, etc.

"Actually just two weeks after I surrendered to God I was asked to pray for a blind man – and he received his sight again!

Even though we were only teenagers, we began to plant new small congregations at the various educational institutions. Several hundred people became Christians as a result, and many were healed.

Many of my friends from that time are leaders in big churches in Africa today with several thousand members.

## Saw Jesus before him in the flesh

"In 1987, still before I had finished my engineering studies, I was sent out with some other youths as a volunteer evangelist. At that time there was a young man who laid hands on us to give us blessing and power to serve. When that happened, I experienced something very special: I saw Jesus.

I had a burning desire in my heart to see Jesus for myself. I had read about Paul, who was also allowed to see Jesus several years after he had risen from the dead and had ascended into heaven. Why should it be impossible for me to see him, as people throughout the centuries have seen him? I prayed deeply in my heart about it.

I said: 'Lord, I love you with my whole heart.' It wasn't just something I *said*, it was true.

Then the young man laid hands on me, and I saw him in front of me, just as clearly as you are sitting in front of me interviewing me.

*"He just looked at me and said: 'Preach the gospel. Don't get caught up in doctrines... Tell of the good things I have done for them. I will be with you. No illness will be able to stand against you. No demons will be able to stand against you.'*

*The picture is a reconstruction of the face of Jesus - from the famous Shroud of Turin. (www.shroud.com)*

And it wasn't just a vision inside my head or something I imagined – I didn't close my eyes, but I stared straight into Jesus' face.

The tenderness that was in his eyes...

I couldn't endure his presence, it was so powerful that I cried and cried. Now I had seen him whom I had read and heard about. He wasn't just a historic person in a book. I knew that he really was still alive."

## The message from Jesus

"He just looked at me and said:

'Preach the gospel. Don't get caught up in doctrines. Don't get preoccupied by other things. Tell of the good things I have done for them. I will be with you. No illness will be able to stand against you. No demons will be able to stand against you.

If you can make people believe in me and my word, nothing will be impossible. Preach the good news.'"

"That's why I am obedient to his word to me. I have to proclaim it. I have to obey God's word. I am away fourty eight weeks of the year, traveling from place to place all over the world. I love my wife and my children, but I have to pay the price and do what God wants.

It costs everything."

"After Jesus had spoken to me, he did something else for me: He walked right into me so that I fell over like a dead man and cried uncontrollably for hours. I thought I was going to die. My body felt as if it had red hot coals inside it and I was about to explode... I wasn't aware that I was crying. Others told me that afterwards.

When I got up the next morning I didn't know how many hours I had been lying down, and my body was completely confused. But I knew that Jesus was alive. And I didn't need to only preach what I had read about; I had seen him for myself, just as Paul saw him.

Now I understood that Jesus was inside me, and that was what Paul meant when he wrote, "according to his power which is at work in us." (Ephesians 3:20).

## "Like Love walking"

*"What did Jesus look like?"*

"He looked like a Jewish man. He didn't look like most paintings of him. He wasn't a red-headed Irish guy, didn't look very English", laughs Charles.

"No he looked like I had imagined he would, but there was something special about him. It was like seeing love walking. Words can't describe it. But that tenderness that was in him... it was unbelievable. And his eyes – they could see right through you It was like standing naked before him. You couldn't hide anything. He could see everything."

Charles pauses. He is moved just from thinking about that incredible experience of Jesus in the flesh. Shortly afterwards he adds in a quiet voice, as if to direct attention away from himself:

"I have always said that what He did for me, He can do for everyone else as well. He doesn't see any one person as more important than another."

*Charles speaking in Zimbabwe, Africa*

## Faith has to be followed up by action

I read the New testament a lot, and it was incredibly exciting. Suddenly I got clear answers to all the questions I had, and to which no-one had been able to give me credible answers before. And I was angry about the fact that no-one had told me that the Bible contains so many answers to the questions we all struggle with. I felt that religious people had hidden it from me. I was never encouraged to read the Bible for myself when I went to the Catholic church in my hometown. I therefore didn't discover before how clearly the Bible speaks.

At one point, after a week of prayer and fasting, I discovered a new truth: When miracles are recounted, faith was always followed by action. For example, Jesus said to the crippled man: 'Get up and walk!', and he got up and walked. Jesus always taught the people he healed. And his teaching created faith in them.

Until then, we youths had simply prayed for people and hoped that something or other would happen by itself. Every Sunday, for example, we went out to hospitals and prayed for the sick, while at the same time showing them the love we had ourselves received from Jesus."

## Stand up!

"But the following Sunday, after I had understood the new truth about acting in faith, something revolutionarily different happened:

The group I went out with were assigned a ward for dying patients...

I went over to a man who had been lying there waiting to die for four months, and explained to him that Jesus had paid the price for him to be able to become well. I said that if he believed that Jesus had taken his illness, his illness would disappear.

He whispered: *'I believe.'* I prayed for him, and after hesitating briefly I said: 'Stand up!' and I took his hand and pulled him out of bed. He was healed on the spot!

The other twenty or so patients and my fellow students saw it, and started to have more faith, and soon the whole ward were on their feet, rejoicing.

A doctor who came in got very confused and thought he had gone into the wrong ward! But it really *was* the ward for the dying.

The next morning Charles was in Lagos, Nigeria's largest city and former capital, with over eight million people – and lots of slums, disease and crime.

On the street Charles saw a cripple sitting begging, a Muslim man who had been crippled for twelve years after an accident it turned out. Charles really wanted to help the man but didn't have any money on him. Instead he enthusiastically told the man about everything Jesus had done for him. And just like Peter and John did in their day in Acts 3:1-10, he said to the man, 'Look at me! "Silver or gold I do not have, but what I have I give you. In the name of Jesus Christ of Nazareth, walk."

And then he pulled the man to his feet and the man walked. He was really , healed."

## Show them that the gospel works – in the USA as well!

"In 1989 I was on a one week course with the American evangelist T. L. Osborne, who has sparked off the careers of many young preachers. He also prays for the sick and is reputed to have healed more people than anyone else. He is an old man now. When I heard him, my heart burned to reach the whole world with the gospel.

At one point I heard T. L. Osborne say, that God sent him to Africa to show us that the gospel also worked here.

Inside my head I heard God say to me:

*'You go to the USA and show them that the gospel also works there!'*

I was immediately enthusiastic about the idea, but it was impossible for practical reasons. I argued back and forth with God about how impossible it was. But in just the next year, in 1990, he provided me with the opportunity to go to the USA."

## At university in the USA

Charles Ndifon began to study computer science, first at university in Pennsylvania, and later in New York. He was always among the top in his class; he had a good brain. But it was his encounter with the living Jesus that meant the most to him.

"I had to tell people about all the good things Jesus has done for us."

It didn't take  long before his little group at the university began to experience strong growth. The rumor soon got around that there was an African who healed many people in Jesus' name, and many began to believe in Christianity again when they heard his simple and consistent preaching and saw God's power at work.

Soon Charles and his group began to plant new congregations and hold small and large revival meetings.

When he finished his computer science studies, Charles initially worked in the computer department in a Bank in New York. Then he decided to drop his regular wage and work full-time as an evangelist with no salary except for what was left over from the collections taken at the meetings, once all the expenses were paid. Some Christians decided to give gifts to his ministry, so that he wouldn't have to worry about earning money, and it still works this way today. He doesn't have any set wage. On each occasion, his expenses and the expenses of any co-workers are covered by the church or group who invites them. Sometimes it is a generous church, in other cases – for example when they travel in Africa and India – they make a loss.

But this doesn't worry Charles:

## The Lord looks after the provisions

*"I mean - the Lord spoke to me...."*, he says, as if it was the most natural thing in the world. "The Lord spoke to me and said that I should tell everyone that God can heal and save them, like he does in Africa.

I am confident that if it's God's will, then he will also provide for me. When God gives you a *vision*, he also gives you *provision*.

That's why I wasn't really interested in working for a church or organization. Some people tried to entice me by offering me a high salary, but I said to them: 'Listen here, you can't pay me a salary which is high enough, because my employer is God himself, and no-one is as rich as him. He has said he will provide for me, so why would I be interested in working for people?'

There were others who offered for me to work for them or to speak at their conferences, if I would just refrain from saying this or that, which offended some religious people.

'No', I said. I have to say what I believe. I can't compromise God's word to make people happy."

## An authentic message

"You see, when we preach the gospel, it has to be authentic. If we preach some form of diluted or mixed version, it has no power. Then Christianity loses its power."

*"Do you believe that many ministers today preach a diluted or mixed up message?"*

"I don't want to judge them. I'm not saying they are doing it with any evil

138

*Thousands attend open air meeting in Mexico.*

intent. Many of them are good people with good intentions, but they don't know any better. How can they preach better if they don't know better?

If they knew the message, and really took it seriously, they would also be able to preach powerfully. But they have to know what the Bible says, and they have to believe it. Oh, I do so want to help people to understand what the Bible says."

*"Is that the key?"*

"Simply to believe, that's the key. It's that simple. To believe and follow Jesus."

## Married to Donna

In 1991, Charles married a young American woman, Donna Lynne, and they now have four boys. Their last son was born in March 2000.

But even Charles' wife, Donna Lynne, had trouble believing what her husband was preaching. She had grown up in a traditional Baptist family, where people didn't believe that Jesus heals today. Healings were something that belonged to Bible history.

Often when Charles told her what he believed, she got angry with him and walked away. Charles didn't know that when she got home, she studied her Bible to see if what he was saying was really true. She had never heard it put that way before. But gradually her prejudices were changed.

Donna had a problem in that she was deaf in one ear. Charles often prayed for her, but she doubted that anything could happen. And nothing did happen either.

"Whenever we talked together she would say: 'Eh?'"

One day when Charles got sick of having to always speak to one side of her head, he said:

"Donna, do you believe that God can heal you right now?"

"Yes", she answered. She had by now reached a resolution.

Immediately Charles commanded the deaf spirit to come out of her ear, and immediately she began to hear. Even the scars inside her ear disappeared.

## Donna now teaches about healing as well

"Today our whole family prays for the sick. Even our nine-year-old boy has prayed for a boy in Holland who had a damaged hand and it was healed", says Charles.

"Our children have grown up with healings; it is the most natural thing in the world for them. Even my little four-year-old son can drive out evil spirits. We won't accept them coming to our house."

"Unfortunately I have to be away from my family a lot. But today Donna also assists at some of my healing meetings.

Often when people ask me to speak somewhere in the USA there are lots of other preachers who want to speak at the same conference, so that their name can go on the poster", laughs Charles, with his unfailing African humour.

"But I say, 'Why not use Donna? She can teach on healing too.' I like to take her along on our campaigns. So she sometimes teaches as well. And she also heals the sick."

# Meeting Charles personally

## What's he actually like, in private?

When Charles Ndifon was on Bornholm for a week in January 2002, I took the opportunity to meet the famous "healing preacher" more personally and get to know him better. After all, how famous people behave in front of a big hall full of people is one thing, and how they behave in private is something else.

If one runs through the gallery of "great preachers", you find that many of them have had rather unusual personalities. For example, Kathrine Kuhlmann, who was no doubt the most prominent healing preacher in the USA in the twentieth century, was rumored to have countless shoes and magnificent dresses! Benny Hinn, who is probably the healing preacher who is attracting the most people at the moment, was an admirer of Kathrine Kuhlmann. At his own meetings, the most dramatic manifestations take place, and Benny Hinn is very theatrical in his behavior. He loves, for example, to lead the singing, and wanders incessantly around the stage with his hair combed over to help cover his bald patch. Morris Cerrullo speaks with a hiss which is reputed to frighten away all the small children, etc.

What was Ndifon like – in real life?

### On the same plane

I contacted Jørgen Christensen, the leader of the Pentecostal church in Rønne, who arranged for me to have as much time as possible with Ndifon.

Pastor Jørgen Christensen was very open about everything and extremely helpful all along the way, without in any way trying to influence what I wrote. I was told, for example, which plane Charles Ndifon was going to arrive on, so that I could catch the same flight from Copenhagen to Rønne, and Jørgen took care of introducing and commending me.

Ndifon flew alone and lugged around his suitcases and oversized hand luggage himself. 'Yes, he's a real African all right', I thought and was reminded of my travels in Africa together with warm and vibrant Africans.

They seem to always have too much luggage they need to squeeze in.

From the airport we drove together in Jørgen's old white Mercedes, after which I checked into the same hotel as Ndifon – Hotel Fredensborg – in Rønne, and was lucky enough to end up staying in a next-door room to his. And it wasn't very long before we were on first name terms and were sitting in the restaurant enjoying a large dinner.

## What a glutton…!

If I had imagined that Charles – as I now called him – was an aesthetic, pious man, who only ate vegetables and fasted most of the time, I would have been quite wrong.

Charles impatiently told the Bornholm waiter that he was so hungry he could eat a horse. But he had been traveling all night too, and if he had looked forward to a good breakfast on Mærsk Air, he would have been just as disappointed as I was. We could choose between apple juice and a bottle of water…

But then Charles found an item on the menu with a sizeable figure beside it and found out from the waiter that it was something involving "steak" and "beef". "OK, I'll take it".

"But that dish can only be served for two people", the waiter apologized, and I had already ordered a more modest dish which wouldn't cause my accountant to raise his eyebrows.

"Don't you think I can handle it?", Charles commented humorously to the waiter. "Just give me the whole roast. I'm hungry, man!"

"Yes of course", replied the waiter and soon afterwards brought out a dish containing a sizeable roast. It was an exclusive dish, and I can assure you that the exquisite meat was prepared so that it was still red inside.

"Oh no", said Charles. "The meat hasn't had enough. Couldn't you cook it a bit more?"

"It's actually meant to look like that", the waiter tried to say patiently, but Charles wanted it cooked better, and the waiter hurriedly packed up the dish, with a slightly wounded comment about it "being a bit late now, but…". However, Charles had soon won over the waiter's heart with his warm African humour.

Some place or other I think it offended my frugal Danish moderation mentality and my sense of personal modesty, that this pious man of God allowed himself to eat so well.

142

But then I recalled that Jesus himself was accused of eating well, "Here is a glutton and a drunkard, a friend of tax collectors and 'sinners'", the Pharisees said (Luke 7:34). At the same time they accused John the Baptist of being demon-possessed because he fasted! There's no pleasing some people.

## When all else fails...

On the other hand, Charles drank neither wine nor spirits, and he doesn't smoke either if that might be a comfort for some people. There is no doubt that he believes smoking destroys the body, and that it therefore can't be God's will for us to smoke.

But Charles is not one to judge anyone.

After having spoken to him for hours on Sunday, I gradually developed a persistent headache. First I tried in vain to sleep. An aspirin/codeine tablet didn't help either, after which I drank a big glass of draught beer, in the hope of getting my body to relax before the evening meeting. But that didn't help either. I'm sure I smelled of beer as we drove together to the Christian meeting in the hall, so I, slightly guiltily, explained to Charles that it was because of

*Charles Ndifon is a very spiritual man - and at the same time a very down-to-earth man. With a good sense of humor which helps the sick to relax.*

144

my throbbing headache. He laughed heartily at my explanations.

At the hall, Jørgen Christensen was already underway telling the many people who had gathered about his big vision for Bornholm. As we stood at the back of the hall and waited for him to introduce Charles, I gathered my courage and asked, "You couldn't just pray for that headache, could you?"

Charles immediately laid his arm around my head and said something like, "I command the headache to disappear. Go!"

It must have only taken five seconds. I still had a headache, but only for two minutes, then it was gone. And the whole evening I had a lovely relaxed feeling in my head. I was completely blissful.

## Assistants and trainees

His volunteer assistants also came to the meetings: This time it was Hans, a young architect from Amsterdam who was a kind of apprentice at the meetings; Mark, a musically gifted minister from Vancouver in Canada, who sometimes leads the singing and plays backing piano at the meetings; and finally Pastor Dail, a black American minister who assists in praying for the sick. Dale was the last one to arrive because he missed a flight in the USA.

Charles Ndifon told me that he regularly offered people who were interested to come along on campaigns around the world, so that they could

*Canadian Mark Cole (left) singing "God is my rock!" and American pastor Dail Jordan - two of Charles Ndifon's close assistants*

learn themselves how to pray for the sick. And as we talked about it, he immediately encouraged me to come along to Zimbabwe where the next "crusade" was going to take place. He was already quite sure that the healings there would surpass what I could manage to see in Europe.

"In Africa people are much more open towards miracles, and they don't have any choice… If they don't get healed, there are generally no doctors or social services who will look after them." So they come full of faith and expectation, and the most fantastic miracles happen", Charles confided in me.

Over the next few days we spent a lot of time together, talking for hours. For example, we always ate together, and I was allowed to let my little tape recorder record our conversations so that I could write them down later.

*Hans, a young architect from Amsterdam who was a kind of apprentice at the meetings, was asked to pray for an old lady's legs*

146

# The woman at his side

Donna Ndifon is not just "the woman behind Ndifon"
- she is more accurately "the woman at his side"...
And she has a strong message for modern women.


Donna was born in Hilltown, a small town in Pennsylvania. She was one of the most capable students in her class at high school, and studied biology and chemistry at college. She planned to become a veterinarian, but then she met Charles and her life was dramatically changed.

*"When did you meet Charles for the first time?"*

"At college."

*"Why did you marry Charles?"*

"I married Charles because I love him, and because he was the first man I have met who was a true Christian. I promised myself at an early age that I would only marry a man who truly loved God with his whole heart and who lived his life consistently with that. I therefore never went out with anyone on a date. I couldn't be bothered wasting time on something which didn't lead anywhere anyway."

*"But how could you know that?"*

"You just need to watch and listen. The way a person behaves and talks shows what they believe. What the heart is filled with, the mouth overflows with.

It's a big problem today that so many just throw themselves at the first and best person because they are so lonely. And later they can't understand why they have so many problems in their relationship. If they just knew what they wanted, and realized that they themselves are worth waiting for, they wouldn't need to be in such a hurry. They could save themselves a lot of grief."

*"You had a problem when you met Charles...?"*

"Yes, when we met, I was partially deaf in one ear due to an injury a doctor had caused when I was a child. I had always believed in Jesus, but I didn't know that he hadn't just taken my sins, but also my sicknesses. When I first began to believe it, I was immediately healed. Since that happened, I have consciously tried to share that knowledge with everyone."

*"You sign your name as 'Pastor Donna Ndifon' – do you also serve as a pastor?"* I asked Donna Ndifon.

"Yes, I am a pastor in our own church here on Rhode Island. It's called *Providence Miracle Center*. It's here that we plant the seeds for everything that's happening around the world."

*"Do you also heal the sick?"*

"The gospel works for everyone, if he or she will just believe. Charles and I have worked together for nearly twelve years. I have been to Holland, Australia, Zimbabwe, the Virgin Islands and several places all over the USA and Canada.

Everywhere, God has confirmed his word with miracles and healings. For example, during our last visit to Zimbabwe I held many women's meetings and also preached during the campaign alongside Charles. Hundreds of people were miraculously healed at these meetings. At the women's meetings, the queue of women coming up to tell of their healings was so long that it continued down the middle aisle of the hall.

The lame jumped and danced, the blind could see again, the deaf could hear... A woman had had heart problems which caused her stomach to swell up. The swelling disappeared in an instant, and she said that her skirt had suddenly become to big. An elderly lady had been blind in one eye since birth. When I commanded the blind spirit to leave her, she began to see immediately!

*"Why are these extraordinary things happening?"*

"It's not because I'm Charles Ndifon's wife, and it's not because I have any special talents or gifts. It's because Jesus is alive and HE is the healer. I'm just a person who has chosen to believe that when Jesus says that 'these signs will accompany those who believe... they will place their hands on sick people, and they will get well' (Mark 16:17), that it also includes me."

## Their children heal as well

Donna and Charles have four boys: Charles Jr. who is nine, Philip who is eight, Paul who is five, and little Jesse who is just two years old.

*"Is it true that your children also pray for the sick?"*

"Our children preach as well, and the miracles follow. Our eldest son, Charles Jr., met a boy in Holland on our campaign there last year. The boy had a broken finger. Charles Jr. asked the boy to take off his splint and clench

*"I married Charles because I love him, and because he was the first man I have met who was a true Christian."*

his fist. The boy did so, and pain shot through his arm, so he began to walk away. But Charles Jr. stopped him and asked him to do it again. He did it again, and the pain was still there. Charles then took the boy's hand and commanded the pain to go away. Then he asked the boy to clench his fist again. He did, and this time the pain was gone. The boy came afterwards and testified that the pain was completely gone. He cried that evening because he so much wanted to talk to Charles Jr. but he could only speak Dutch, and Charles Jr. couldn't. But God's power had still been able to move freely despite the language difficulties.

When he was only eighteen months old, our third son, Paul, crawled up to a lady who was so sick that she didn't have the strength to move. He blew on her face. She immediately drew herself up, shocked over what had happened. When he blew on her, God's power had gone through her body, and she immediately gained strength in her body.

It doesn't matter to God who you are. You're never too young or too old for God to use you. The only thing you have to do is believe.

## We all want to help people

*"Isn't it difficult for you that Charles travels around the world so much?"*

"People ask me that all the time, and the answer is simple: No, because we both share the same vision – to spread the good news about what Jesus has done for ALL people in the whole world. Both I and our children are driven by the same passion to help people. I get a rich reward when Charles calls me on the phone and tells me about all the people who have been healed and set free. The key is focus. As long as we focus on the goal and keep our eyes fixed on Jesus, all other things fall into their rightful place.

*"What's Charles like as a husband and father?"*

"What can I say? He is simply the best husband in the world. He has always inspired me to become everything which God has created me to be. He has never felt threatened by my success, but rather has always encouraged me to strive for even more.

He is also like this towards the children – always inspiring, always encouraging them to have big dreams and always teaching them never to give up seeking the best God has for them. He is very loving, compassionate and strong. I thank God for him every day.

## God wants to use women

*"Do you have a word for the women?"*

"My word to all women is: *God's word.*

God believes in women. The first preacher in the Bible was a woman. That was Eve. When the Devil tempted them, it was Eve who protested and said, "God has said…". Adam didn't say anything. The first person to preach the gospel about Jesus was also a woman: Mary Magdalene. Jesus revealed himself to her after the resurrection and told her to go to the others and tell them the good news that he had risen from the dead.

God uses women in the same way he uses men. All that he needs is for the person to be willing to do his bidding. For far too long 'Christ's body' (the church) has suffered from a stroke. Half of the body has been paralyzed by religion and human traditions. We only use half of the body's energy and potential, so it's no wonder that the church only does half of the work it should be doing.

But you will be pleased to know that Christ's body (the church) has begun to function. The paralysis is disappearing and the body is almost running on all cylinders again. Women everywhere are realizing that they also have their destiny in Christ – that they also have a job to do here on earth – in addition to being a good wife and mother. It's time now for women to stand up and take their rightful place beside the men in order to reach out to this suffering world. God created man and woman to rule over the earth together – not over each other (read Genesis 1:26-27). He later divided the two so that they could help each other to take care of tasks. The whole idea with salvation

*A woman is having her left ear healed: While the helper holds a finger in her right ear, so she can't hear anything, pastor Charles speaks softly into her deaf ear. When she begins to hear, Charles moves away – still speaking softly. And her deaf ear can still hear... She is healed. This happens very often.*

was to bring us back to God's original plan.

So put briefly, my advice to women is, "Throw off all the limitations placed on you. Forget the past. Forget your poor excuses – and see yourselves just as God sees you, and then – get going!"

*"What do you think of everything that's happening in the meetings?"*

"I'm so happy about what's happening. What makes me happiest is all the people who have indicated that they are going to give their hearts and lives to Jesus Christ. He is the only answer to people's suffering and problems. There is nothing better than to have the "answer" to all of life's problems living *inside you*.

That's the biggest miracle.

When your body, soul and mind are healed, it's the result of the fact that the big *Healer* has come inside you and lives in you.

# What Donna and Charles believe:

## (and Christ Love Ministries International)

We believe in the unchanging God who made the heavens and the earth.

We believe that Jesus Christ is God's Son (Mt 16:16; Jn 1:49; Jn 3:35-36) Conceived of the Holy Spirit (Lk 1:34-37);

Born of a virgin (Is 7:14: Mt 1:23)

Who came as God in the flesh (Jn 1:14; 14:6-11; Rom 8:3; I Tim3:16)

Who bore our sins for us in His death on the Cross (I Pet 2:24; Is. 53:3-5)

Who shed His blood for the remission of our sins (Mt 26:28; Eph 1:7)

Who died for us and was raised from the dead for our justification (I Cor. 15:4 ; Rom 4:25)

Who is now seated at God's right hand (Eph. 1:20, Heb. 1012; Heb. 12:2; Col. 3:1)

Who forever makes intercession for us. (Heb. 7:25; I Tim. 2:5)

We believe the Bible is the infallible revelation of God's love plan for a hurting world.

We believe in the power of the Holy Spirit at work in the believers today. (Acts 1:8)

We believe that a true believer does the works of Jesus Christ today (Jn. 14:12; Mt 4:23-25)

We believe that Jesus Christ is the same, yesterday, today and forever (Heb. 13:8)

We believe there is only one true Church – the body of Christ (1Cor. 12:27; 1 Cor. 3:11; Eph 4:4-6)

We believe in the great commission to reach the world with the Gospel of Jesus Christ.

We believe in peace with God, peace from God through Christ Jesus.

We believe in Miracles, because God is the God of Miracles!!!

We believe in the strength of the local body of believers called the Church an assembly of the saints.

# Questions and answers

## What's the secret Charles...?

*"What is the key to experiencing a life full of power as you have"*, I asked Charles Ndifon as we sat in the Hotel Fredensborg restaurant and spoke loudly about God and Jesus.

"Read the Bible and believe what it says", he answers.

*"But that almost sounds too easy... And reading the Bible and believing it – there are many of us who believe we are already doing that..."*

"Yes, but it's about getting back to basics. "Read the book *without filters*, without all the theological interpretations and doctrines which get in the way", answers Charles Ndifon.

"It's rarely a problem for people who are not Christians beforehand. They go straight to the Bible text without reservation, but for many Christians its a problem because they have already been indoctrinated to not believe or understand what they read, because of their religious prejudices.

Many Christians say to me: 'I believe the Bible, but...'

There is always a 'but'.

But, but, but.

All these 'but's' are about doubting God. So I say to them: Do you think your God is a liar?

The Bible says God CAN'T lie." [1]

## Don't just pray, heal!

*"But who should pray for the sick? Is it something which all Christians can and should do – or is it only something for a chosen few?"*

"We shouldn't just *pray* for the sick. We should *heal* the sick. Many sick people have had enough prayers, their faith has been prayed to death. They just need to be healed.

God isn't deaf. We don't need to pray again and again. Jesus said: 'Father, I know that you always hear me.' It's like that for us too. God hears us.

*"But who then should heal the sick?"*

"It's simple enough: *All Christians*. After all, Jesus says: 'Heal the sick!'"

*"Yes, but perhaps he was just speaking to the disciples?"*

"I have to smile, because the New Testament says that there was also a man who didn't belong to the twelve disciples who went around healing in Jesus name. And Jesus said that they shouldn't stop him."

(John said, "Master, we saw a man driving out demons in your name and we tried to stop him, because he is not one of us." "Do not stop him", Jesus said, "for whoever is not against you is for you." - Luke 9:49-150)

"The problem is often that the people who look like they know a lot about that type of question don't know the Bible themselves. They have their theology, and they teach people that you shouldn't do what Jesus says after all. And the result is weak churches and self-contradictory preaching which is no use for anything."

## A question of authority

*"But couldn't it be that some have a special gift? A spiritual gift. That you, for example have a gift to heal is clear."*

"Yes, it is a gift, but it is available to everyone who believes. It's not something I'm making up. The Bible says so. *The anointing* is for everyone who believes, but the authority varies. You grow by using your gift. The power is the same, but we have different levels of authority.

A police officer and a police commissioner exercise the same power, but they have different levels of authority. It's the same. God gives authority, but we grow in it. Some don't grow because they want to raise the dead but don't want to heal headaches.

## Definition: Anointing

There are several examples in the Old Testament of a new king or prophet being anointed with olive oil as a visible sign that God's spirit was upon them. In the New Testament oil is again a sign of the Spirit, the Holy Spirit.

For example, John writes, "But you have an *anointing* from the Holy One, and all of you know the truth" (1 John 2:20) . And later in verse 27:

"As for you, the *anointing* you received from him remains in you, and you do not need anyone to teach you. But as his *anointing* teaches you about all things and as that anointing is real, not counterfeit - just as it has taught you, remain in him."

There is no doubt that John is referring to the Holy Spirit here when he talks about an anointing which believers have.

## Oil is used as a symbol of the Holy Spirit

When Jesus sends out the twelve disciples to try out his power – while he is still on earth, before he sends them out in earnest at the time of his ascension and on the day of Pentecost – it is written about them:

"They went out and preached that people should repent. They drove out many demons and *anointed many sick people with oil* and healed them." (Mark 6:12-13).

Later James described in his letter how the leaders in the congregation should use oil as a sign of the Holy Spirit when interceding for the sick:

"... Is any one of you sick? He should call the elders of the church to pray over him and anoint him with oil in the name of the Lord. And the prayer offered in faith will make the sick person well; the Lord will raise him up. If he has sinned, he will be forgiven." (James 5:14-15)

The oil (the anointing) is thus a symbol of the Holy Spirit. And Jesus tells the leader of the church at Laodicea, that he should buy "salve to put on your eyes, so you can see". And it's clear from the context that he's not talking about eye drops, but the fact that the man needs to be filled with the Holy Spirit so that he can see spiritually clearly. It says:

"You say: 'I am rich; I have acquired wealth and do not need a thing.' But you do not realize that you are wretched, pitiful, poor, blind and naked. I counsel you to buy from me gold refined in the fire, so you can become rich; and white clothes to wear, so you can cover your shameful nakedness; and salve to put on your eyes, so you can see." (Revelation 3:17-18)

## All believers can use the gifts

When Ndifon talks about "the anointing" being for all Christians, he means that the fullness of the Holy Spirit is *available* to all Christians, and with the Holy Spirit, the spiritual gifts – like being able to heal – which are discussed in 1 Corinthians 12. Everyone who is filled with the Holy Spirit has authority to use the gifts. But, he points out, the authority varies. By authority he means "the right to use the power". Only when you use the power do you grow in authority and become able to make ever greater use of the spiritual gifts.

## Disappointment

*"Perhaps the reservations some people have about praying for the sick are due to the fact that they have been disappointed before?"*

155

"Yes, for example if you've had a case in the church where you prayed for someone who then died, the church might think: 'We'd better completely abandon praying for the sick.'

But the same church wouldn't stop preaching the gospel, even if some people didn't receive it and they died and went to Hell, unforgiven. They would still keep preaching.

In the same way, it's not logical either to stop praying for the sick just because not everyone gets well."

*"But surely even some of the people you pray for don't get healed...?"*

"The critical thing is whether people are willing to change their *lifestyle*. If a person has cancer and I heal him in Jesus name, and he then goes home and continues to smoke like a chimney, then he's not serious is he. It would seem he just wants to be healed in order to destroy himself again and serve the Devil even better..."

## The churches have to follow up on it

*"There are actually a number of people who were apparently healed on your last tour, but who don't want to have anything to do with church...?"*

"No, and part of the problem is that the churches don't preach the way we do. I think many would come to the churches if they continued to preach in the same way that I do. You can read about this in 1 Corinthians 15. People have to be able to see that something is happening; that the message has consequences.

Often some people are healed at a meeting, and then I get invited to speak at their home church. But if that church doesn't preach the message afterwards, it all collapses again.

If the ministers don't know what they should say, then I'm very happy to send them a cassette with a sermon. When I had to preach for the first time myself, I had to learn what the apostle Peter preached so that I could re-use his sermon. I just changed the name of the town!

But many people are so arrogant that they won't just preach the words of the Bible, or what someone else has preached; they want to add their own thoughts, and then they botch things up."

## Those who lose their healing

*"Some of the people who were healed during your last tour have 'lost their healing' after some time. Why does that happen?"*

"When you are healed, you have to make sure to fill your life with what can keep you healthy. You have to begin to live as the Bible teaches us. From the same place which healing comes from, comes also that which can keep you healthy.

Some people come back to my meetings and say: 'Oh, now I'm sick again.' And then I ask them: 'But did you do what I said to do?'

Some have cancer but continue to smoke. It's like when you go to a doctor – if it doesn't work, you come back for more treatment. And the doctor also says: 'Stop smoking'.

But many people say: 'No, I can't give up my cigarettes.' OK, then stay sick...

A big problem in the West is laziness. When the government pays everything for you, there are some who won't give up their sickness. They don't want to lose their disabled pension or the special social services. Healing means you have to get up and walk, you have to start working. That's not always so comfortable.

We don't have that problem in Africa. People don't get any money from the government there, because the government has no money. So for them it's necessary to be healed in order to live. If they can't work they're finished."

*"What about mental illnesses – are they harder to heal?"*

"No, they're just the same as the physical illnesses. We have healed lots of maniacs."

*"But what goes wrong when someone doesn't get healed?"*

"If I pray for someone and they don't get healed, I don't look to God and ask why he didn't do it. I don't even look at the person who didn't get healed. I look at myself and ask: 'What did I do wrong?' I must have missed something. Let me try again.

Some American pastors don't dare to heal the sick. They ask me: 'What should we do with the people who don't get healed?' And I smile and say: 'What do you do with the people who don't accept the gospel and get saved?'"

*"You talk about healing and salvation as if they are the same thing?"*

"Yes, when I preach to non-Christians they see that Jesus heals, and so they believe in Jesus. They are the same thing for them. But we Christians who have grown up in Christian churches have been taught that salvation and healing are two different things. But if you look at the scriptures, the word which is used for saved and healed is the same word in Greek: sōzō.[2]

*"But the church divides it up – why?"*

157

"Because many people don't know how to handle the power."

They often only preach about being saved for eternity, about going to heaven. But what about salvation here and now? Doesn't Christianity have anything to say about life here and now? Yes, lots, but you have to read what is actually written in the Bible – without theological filters.

But the big problem is that many people think they believe. They say they believe the Bible. But when it comes to the crunch, they say "but... um.."

*"But are you sure that everyone can be healed?"*

"Is it God's word that he wants everyone to be saved?

*"Yes. For example, in 1 Timothy 2:3-4 it says '...God our Savior... wants all men to be saved and to come to a knowledge of the truth.'"*

"OK, there's your answer: If God wants to save everyone from their sins, then he also wants to heal them from their illnesses."

*"So you have no reservations?"*

"No!" says Charles firmly. "It's good news for everyone."

*"But what about people who don't believe? Can they be healed?"*

"They will start believing when they see it works. Do you know why they didn't believe? Because no one had told them the good news."

*"But what if someone says: 'I want to be healed, but I don't want to be a Christian?'"*

"No problem. I say: 'If you get healed now, will you believe that Jesus is alive?'

There was a man in Odense who came to me and said: 'I don't believe in this.' He was a tough case, but whenever I see a tough case I think to myself, 'he's tough because it hurts inside.'

So he wouldn't believe. And I asked him: 'If you get healed now, will you believe it and turn to the Lord?' 'Yes', he said. So I just said: 'Father, touch him' – and immediately he was healed.

'You gave me your word', I said to him. 'You said you would believe and turn to the Lord. Now you have to do it.' And he did.

Jesus also encountered people who wouldn't believe before they saw a sign. I have encountered thousands of cases like that.

Sometimes people come up and say that they don't believe it. Sometimes they even curse and swear after they have been healed, because they are used to speaking that way.

When they can't understand that they have been healed, they sometimes exclaim: 'What the hell has happened?' It doesn't bother me. They're just so surprised."

## Healers and magicians

*"It is claimed that some so-called healers can also perform healings. Even though they don't use Jesus' name. What do you say to that?"*

"In Odense a 'healer' came to me and said: 'I do the same thing you do – I heal as well. I can heal myself.' So I asked him: 'Then why have you come here?' He said: 'I just need a bit of help.' But I said to him: 'I know that you can't heal yourself. Prove that you can.' And then I went on to the next person. That was in the middle of the meeting.

Later I came back to him and he admitted that he couldn't. So I told him: 'My friend, listen, you can't heal yourself. Only God can do it. You must confess your sin and turn to God immediately.' And do you know what? He prayed with one of my assistants and afterwards I healed him on the spot.

People often come to me and say that they can heal. And I'm not just polite, saying:

'That's very interesting.' No, I know that they can't heal. We also have witchdoctors in Africa, and I know what they can and what they can't do. They are often friendly people, and they try to help people too, but they have limited power.

The power they have and use is the power of seduction. They can do conjuring tricks. Magic."

## Seriously religious Indians

"In India thirty thousand people had gathered to hear me speak. Many were Hindus, and others were Muslims. I had noticed all their temples and could see that they were very religious. I said: 'You are wonderful people. You are seeking God.' I wouldn't judge them as many people would have done, because I wanted to show them that God is living."

*"What was the reaction from the Indians?"*

"Well, fifteen thousand wanted to become Christian, so I guess you can say that the reaction was positive", laughs Charles.

"But the Indians told me that the gurus could heal. Even the Christians believed it, because they didn't have power themselves. But I told them that the gurus can't heal. They can't open the eyes of the blind, or make the deaf hear. Those kinds of things are the signs of the Messiah. Demons can perform miracles, but they can't heal. They can call down fire, they can make a chair move, they can make pain disappear, but show me a cripple who has walked, a blind man who can now see or a deaf man who can now hear. Only God can do the works which Jesus did, and which we can do in His name.

The kind of healers and witchdoctors who don't work in Jesus name use the spirit of seduction. They get people to believe that they are healed even though they are still sick.

In the USA they want to use music in the background to create a mood, but I actually prefer not to use that kind of thing. I don't see why we need to create a mood. If the power is real, it will work whether there is a mood or not. If not, then I'd better go back to working as an engineer again. We don't need to manipulate people."

## People who saw Jesus

*"It is claimed that some people have seen Jesus at your meetings...?"*

"We experience so many incredible things at our meetings that we have given up trying to keep track of them and record them. The only thing we do is video all the meetings.

But I remember, for example, from the first meetings in Copenhagen that there was a woman who really saw Jesus walk past her during the meeting. She was so sure that she saw Jesus that she shouted loudly over in one corner: 'No Jesus, don't walk past me!'

Then she saw Jesus turn around and stand still, while he looked at her with a strong gaze. She called to him, and he came towards her and she became well...

That highlights for me what I have experienced so often, that Jesus never pushes himself on you.

Once in Canada there were forty people who all saw Jesus walking around during a meeting. I was puzzled about why people weren't looking at me, and why miracles were happening around the hall. But it was Jesus who was going around healing.

It has also happened a few times that people at the meetings have been able to see a light around me, even though I couldn't see it myself."

Notes:
1 E.g. "He who is the Glory of Israel does not lie or change his mind; for he is not a man, that he should change his mind." 1 Samuel 15:29.
2 See the following chapters which deals with the subject: Salvation = Healing in more detail.
3 In the beginning of February 2002, the TV-Avisen news program exposed the fact that guru Sai Baba's so-called miracles were in reality conjuring tricks.

# God wants you well

Using quotes from the Bible, Charles Ndifon points out that healing is within salvation. *Comments in italic.*

## (I) Healing is in the word

**Proverbs 4:20-22:** My son attend to my words: incline thine ear unto my sayings. Let them not depart from thine eyes: keep them in the midst of thine heart. For they are Life unto those that find them, and Health (Medicine) to all their flesh

**Psalms 107:20:** He sent His word, and healed them, and delivered them from their destructions.

**John 1:1, 14:** In the beginning was the Word, and the Word was with God, and the Word was God and the Word was made flesh and dwelt among us..

**Romans 10:17:** Faith comes by hearing God's word.

**Hosea 4:6:** My people are destroyed for lack of knowledge... seeing you have forgotten the law of thy God. *Obedience to the word brings healing.*

## (II) Healing is in Redemption!

**Isaiah 53:4, 5:** Surely He has borne our griefs [*sicknesses*], and carried our sorrows [*pains, diseases*]: yet we did esteem Him stricken, smitten of God, and afflicted. And with his stripes [bruises] we are healed.

**Matthew 8:16, 17:** And healed all that were sick; that it might be fulfilled which was spoken by Isaiah the prophet, saying, He himself took our infirmities, and bore our sicknesses.

**1 Peter 2:24:** Who his own self bore our sins in His own body on the tree. That we, being dead to sins should live unto righteousness: by whose stripes you were healed.

*Were healed - past tense! If you were healed then you are healed! Jesus Christ bore our sicknesses, why should we bear them? If you were healed 2,000 years ago then you are healed! Jesus purchased your healing 2,000 years ago. You only need to receive it. Just like salvation! Healing is in God's redemptive plan.*

**Galations 3:13:** Christ has redeemed us from the curse of the law, being

161

made a curse for us: for it is written, cursed is every one that hangeth on a tree.

*What's the curse of the law? Poverty, sickness, death! Christ has redeemed us from the curse!*

**Psalms 103:2, 3:** Bless the Lord, O my soul, and forget not all his benefits: Who forgiveth all thine iniquities; who healeth all thy diseases;

**Ex. 23:25:** ...I will take sickness away from the midst of thee.

**Ex. 15:26:** If you will diligently hearken to the voice of the Lord your God, and will do that which is right in His sight, and will give ear to His commandments, and keep all His statutes, I will put [permit, allow] none of these diseases upon thee, which I have brought upon the Egyptians; for I am the Lord that healeth thee. - *I am, not I was!*

**Malachi 3:6:** I am the Lord I change not. *God doesn't change!*

**Hebrews 8:6:** *says that we have a better covenant based upon better promises.*

## (III) It is God's will to heal you!

**1 John 5:14, 15:** This is the confidence we have in approaching God: that if we ask anything according to His will, He hears us. And if we know that He hears us—whatever we ask—we know that we have what we asked of Him.

*Jesus is the expression of the father's will.*

**Hebrews 1:3:** Jesus being the brightness of His glory, and the express image of His person...

**Hebrews 13:8:** Jesus Christ is the same yesterday, and today, and forever.

*He healed then, He'll heal now!*

## (IV) God is the healer!

*The devil is the destroyer!*

**John 10:10:** The thief comes only to steal and kill and destroy..... *But Jesus came to destroy the destroyer!*

**1 John 3:8:** For this purpose the son of God was manifested *(revealed)*, that He might destroy the works of the devil.

**John 10:10:** ...I have come that they might have life, and that they might have it more abundantly.

## (V) Healing is for all!

**Matt. 12:15:** ...And Jesus healed them all.

**Matt 14:35, 36** ...And brought unto Him all that were diseased: And besought Him that they might only touch the hem of His garment; and as many as touched were made perfectly whole.

*As many as touched Him!*

**Luke 4:40:** ...All they that had any sick with diverse diseases brought them unto Him; and He laid His hands on every one of them, and healed them.

**Luke 6:19:** And the whole multitude sought to touch Him; for there went virtue out of Him, and healed them all.

**Acts 10:38:** How God anointed Jesus of Nazareth with the Holy Ghost and with power; who went about doing good and healing all that were oppressed of the devil; for God was with Him.

*God is no respecter of persons.*

**Acts 10:34:** *He healed them, He will heal you!*

**James 5:14-16:** Is anyone sick among you? Let him call for the elders of the church; and let them pray over him, anointing him with oil in the name of the Lord; And the prayer of faith shall save *(heal)* the sick, and the Lord shall raise him up; and if he have committed sins, they shall be forgiven him. Confess your faults one to another, and pray one for another, that you may be healed. The effectual fervent prayer of a righteous man avails much.

## (VI) For ministers only? NO!

**John 14:12:** ...He that believes on me *(Jesus)*, the works that I do shall he do also; and greater works than these shall he do; because I go unto my father.

*Believers get to work! Jesus said we would do greater works!*

**Acts 3:6-8:** Then Peter said, silver and gold have I none; but such as I have give I thee; in the name of Jesus Christ of Nazareth rise up and walk. And He took him by the right hand, and lifted him up; and immediately his feet and ankle bones received strength. And he leaping up stood, and walked, and entered with them into the temple, walking, and leaping, and praising God.

**Acts 8:5-8:** Then Philip went down to the city of Samaria, and preached Christ unto them. And the people with one accord gave heed unto those things which Philip spoke, hearing and seeing the miracles which He did. For unclean spirits, crying with loud voice, came out of many that were possessed with them; and many taken with palsies, and that were lame, were healed. And there was great joy in that city.

*Believers do the works of Jesus!*

**Acts 14:7-10:** And there they preached the gospel. And there sat a certain man at Lystra, impotent in his feet, being a cripple from his mother's womb, who had never walked: The same heard Paul speak; who steadfastly beholding him, and perceiving that he had faith to be healed. Said with a loud voice, stand upright on thy feet. And he leaped and walked.

*They preached the gospel, the man heard Paul speak, faith comes by hearing God's word, they must have preached healing in their gospel message, because the man got healed!*

**Mark 16:17-18:** And these signs shall follow them that believe; in my name... They shall lay hands on the sick and they shall recover.

*If you are a believer, Jesus said you will lay hands on sick people and they will get well!*

## (VII) The Holy Spirit is the power!

**1 John 4:4:** Greater is He that is in you *(Holy Spirit)*, than he that is in the world *(Satan)*.

**Romans 8:11:** But if the spirit of Him that raised up Jesus from the dead dwells in you, He that raised up Christ from the dead shall also quicken your mortal bodies by His Spirit that dwells in you.

*If you are born-again, then the Holy Spirit lives inside you! You have the life-giving power living inside and He quickens or gives life to, or makes alive, your mortal bodies! You must receive and believe the word of God. It must become real for you or it won't work! Get God's word down in your spirit man for it's only what you know and act upon for yourself that counts!*

*Salvation is a gift! (Ephesians 2:8-9)*

*The Baptism in the Holy Spirit is a gift. (Acts 2:38)*

## (VIII) Healing is a gift!

*It's free! It's already been paid for!*

*Accept it! Receive it for yourself and then go and heal others!*

*It's time for the true church of Jesus Christ to go from the mentality of 'I can receive healing for myself if I can just touch the hem of His garment, like the woman with the issue of blood,' to the mentality of 'I can pray for others and they'll get healed because the almighty power of God lives inside me and flows through me to the needy when I pray!'*

*Touch - lay hands on the sick. Command - in Jesus' name . Action - on part of the candidate.*

Note: Different translations are used.

164

# Salvation = healing?

**Are salvation and healing two sides of the same thing? It's time to "search the scriptures"...**

In the chapter entitled "Questions and answers", Charles Ndifon claims that the Greek word which is used for salvation in the New Testament, i.e.: Sōzō, is the same word which is most frequently used for healing. And that the theological division into two concepts is due to the fact that "many people don't know how to handle the power."

After my conversation with Ndifon I looked up whether it was really true that the same Greek word is used for both healing and salvation. And it's actually true. Other words are also used for healing. But these words are also used for salvation from sin. The New Testament doesn't have the great divide between salvation and healing which has developed in theology.

## Salvation = healing

The first time the word 'save' is used in the New Testament is in Matthew 9:21, where a woman who had suffered from bleeding for twelve years approached Jesus from behind and touched the hem of His cloak. v21: "She said to herself, "If I only touch His cloak, I will be healed (sōthēsomai)." v22: Jesus turned and saw her. "Take heart, daughter," he said, "your faith has healed (sesokèn) you." And the woman was healed (ēsothē) from that moment.

Even though the woman here was healed in a physical sense and not just a spiritual one, the word 'saved' is used. The words which are used for 'saved' in these three places are all inflections of the word sōzō, which means rescue, salvage, save.

## A central word in New Testament Christianity

Sōzō is the most commonly used word for salvation/healing in the New Testament. The list below shows where the word appears:

In **Matthew**: 1:21, 8:25, 9:21, 9:22, 10:22, 14:30, 16:25,18:11, 19:25, 24:13, 24:22, 27:40, 27:42, 27:49,

In **Mark**: 3:4, 5:23, 5:28,5:34, 6:56, 8:35, 10:26, 10:52, 13:13, 13:20, 15:30, 15:31, 16:16,

In **Luke**: 6:9, 7:50, 8:12, 8:36, 8:48, 8:50, 9:24, 9:56,13:23, 17:19, 17:33, 18:26, 18:42, 19:10, 23:35, 23:37, 23:39,

In **John**: 3:17, 5:34,10:9, 11:12,12:27, 12:47,

In **Acts**: 2:21, 2:40, 2:47, 4:9, 4:12, 11:14, 14:9, 15:1, 15:11, 16:30, 16:31, 27:20, 27:31,

In **Romans**: 5:9, 5:10, 8:24, 9:27, 10:9, 10:13, 11:14, 11:26,

In **1 Corinthians**: 1:18, 1:21, 3:15, 5:5, 7:16, 9:22, 10:33, 15:2,

In **2 Corinthians**: 2:15 In **Ephesians**: 2:5, 2:8,

In **1 Thessalonians**: 2:16, In **2 Thessalonians**: 2:10,

In **1 Timothy**: 1:15, 2:4, 2:15,4:16, In **2 Timothy**: 1:9, 4:18,

In **Titus**: 3:5, In **Hebrews**: 5:7, 7:25,

In **James**: 1:21, 2:14, 4:12, 5:15, 5:20, In **1 Peter**: 3:21, 4:18,

In **Jude**: 5, 23, In **Revelation**: 21:24.

## Another word for physical healing: To cure

But in a number of places another word is used for healing, that is, *iaomai*, which means *to heal, to cure.*

It is used for the first time in Matthew 8:8 where a Roman officer says: "Lord, I do not deserve to have you come under my roof. But just say the word, and my servant will be healed (*iathēsetai*)." and in v. 13, "And his servant was healed (*iáthē*) at that very hour." (Or: "within the hour".) This word for healing is used in the following places in the New Testament:

In **Matthew**: 8:8, 8:13, 13:15, 15:28,

In **Mark**: 5:29, In **Luke**: 4:18, 5:17, 6:17, 6:17, 6:19 7:7, 8:47, 9:2, 9:11, 9:42, 14:4, 17:15, 22:51,

In **John**: 4:47, 5:13,1, 12:40, In **Acts**: 3:11, 9:34, 10:38, 28:8, 28:27

In **Hebrews**: 12:13, In **James**: 5:16, In **1 Peter**: 2:24.

## Luke, the doctor, used the medical expression

It is especially Luke who uses this word for healing, *to cure*, a total of 17 times in his writings (Luke and Acts).

My Study Bible[1] tells me that the noun *iama / i'ama*, which means healing, is also used three times by Paul in connection with spiritual gifts, see 1 Corinthians 12:9,28,30. He is referring here to a supernatural gift for bringing healing to sick people by prayer and faith. (i.e. the same form of healing which Charles Ndifon practices).

The word is related to the verb, *i'aomai*, to heal, and occurs twenty eight times in the NT – twenty five of which are in the gospels and Acts.

The interesting thing is that this perhaps more medical word for healing, *i'aomai*, is also used to refer to what one could call *spiritual healing*, that is, what theologians normally understand by salvation (i.e. from sin).

This happens in the Bible verses mentioned below:

**Matthew 13:15:** For this people's heart has become calloused; they hardly hear with their ears, and they have closed their eyes.

Otherwise they might see with their eyes, hear with their ears, understand with their hearts and turn, and I would *heal* them.

**Luke 4:18** The Spirit of the Lord is on me, because He has anointed me to preach good news to the poor. *(Here a whole sentence is missing in the NIV and other translations, namely: He sent me to heal those depressed in their hearts.)*

He has sent me to proclaim freedom for the prisoners and recovery of sight for the blind, to release the oppressed *(literally: afflicted)*,

**Acts. 28:27** (same quote as in Mt. 13:15)

**Heb. 12:12-13:** Therefore, strengthen your feeble arms and weak knees. "Make level paths for your feet," so that the lame may not be disabled, but rather *healed*.

**1 Pet. 2:24:** He himself bore our sins in His body on the tree, so that we might die to sins and live for righteousness; by His wounds you have been *healed*.

## "I am the LORD, who heals you."

In the Septuagint Bible translation (from Hebrew to Greek), *i'aomai* is used for the Hebrew word *rafa*, which also means to heal. And it's the same Hebrew word which is used in Exodus 15:26, where God says, "I am the LORD, who heals you."

The word, *i'aomai*, is also used synonymously with *therapévo*, which we know today in the word 'therapy' – it originally meant to *serve*, to take care of. In the New Testament it is used forty four times, but *always in connection with healings*. And it's also the word *therapévo* that Jesus uses when he sends out

167

his twelve disciples and gives them power to heal. .

The text in Luke 9:1-2 says: "When Jesus had called the Twelve together, He gave them power and authority to drive out all demons and to *cure* diseases, and He sent them out to preach the kingdom of God and to heal the sick..."

## Conclusion

So Charles Ndifon is actually right when he says that the division between *spiritual salvation* (from sin – to go to heaven) and *physical healing* (from illness – here and now), which is normally used in theology, is not that reasonable in light of the way the words are used in the New Testament. In the NT, both are normally in play, with salvation and healing being two sides of the same thing.

If one looks back at church history one will also discover that healing didn't just appear among the disciples in Jesus' time, but also later in church history. For example, healings are described by Quadratus, Justin Martyr, Theophilus of Antioch, Ireneaus, Tertullian and Origen.[2] For at least the first three centuries, Christianity was "charismatic".

There are also later accounts of healings and miraculous wonders – for example, when the Christian missionary, Poppo came to Denmark and had to convince King Harald Bluetooth that what he preached was true. In about 965 A.D., Poppo was more or less compelled to take the ordeal by fire – to wear a red-hot iron gauntlet. His hand was not injured – after which Harald Bluetooth was convinced and allowed himself to be baptized – and "made the Danes Christian" as he wrote in runic on the stones at Jelling (below).

Notes:
1 Study Bible I-X, common
Nordic edition
with Greek lexicon, 1988.
2 Evelyn Frost: Christian
Healing, London,
Publisher: AR Mowbray & Co.,
1940

*Even in the time of the Vikings miracles were performed by Christians.*

# Can healings be proven?

**If people really are healed, it must be pretty easy to prove it scientifically. Or is it ?**

Yes, it may be possible to prove healings scientifically, but it's often difficult because there are so many interplaying factors when it comes to changes in an illness. Most people receive some form of treatment or other in the public health system, which can also influence their health. It is therefore difficult to *prove* whether it is prayer or something else which is responsible for any change.

In the USA, in particular, several scientific studies have already been made into the effect of praying for the sick. These show that prayer has a positive effect on the sick.[1] (The most important of these studies will be described later in the book).

## Study of healed persons

Majbrit Andersen, a medical student at Odense University, did carry out a pregraduate study[2] in co-operation with two doctors and an anthropologist. The study was investigating a group of the people who claim that they were healed at the meetings with Charles Ndifon at the *Copenhagen Christian Culture Center* February 21 - 27, 2001.

Over thirty thousand people took part in these meetings, and many have later expressed that they were touched in some way – without it being recorded anywhere. At that point in time, the organizers hadn't thought about the value of following up anyone who was healed in their ongoing lives. They later became aware of this, and now response cards are offered to all participants at all Ndifon's meetings. But there are still many who don't fill these out.

However, at the first meetings in Copenhagen there were two hundred and thirty who filled out response cards, who expressed that they believed they had been healed. And some who expressed that they were not healed.

Majbrit Andersen sent out questionnaires to the addresses of two hundred responsecards which CCCC made available for her investigation.

"Out of all these questionnaires, I eventually received about fifty five back. I started to contact some of those who had not answered and finally got a total of seventy six answers. (38 pct.) Afterward we concluded that the questionnaires were unnecessarily comprehensive and that some of the patients might not have answered because of that. Another reason could have been that I asked them to send the questionnaires back to my personal address."

The response cards did cover all kinds of illnesses from high blood pressure to cancer and HIV. There are people with multiple sclerosis, infertility and mental illnesses. Some have experienced that a lump disappeared. Many have expressed that they have experienced improvement in areas other than their illness. (See the overview on pg. 174).

## 31 out of 76 felt they were still healed after 6 months

Thirteen out of the seventy six are now saying – 6 months afterwards – that they weren't actually healed after all.

Twenty six say that they were well for a period of time, but have since become sick again. (Some have experienced partial healing of one illness, but not another). Some were only well for three-four days, while others have been healthy for up to six months, but now feel that they are sick again. And it cannot only be a psychological effect, because some of the illnesses are very tangible. Some, for example, have been able to *hear* for a period of time, others have had improved *vision* – but only for a certain period. So it's not simply something they have imagined.

"Are there none that have held onto their healing six months afterwards?"

"Yes, there are all of thirty one out of seventy six who indicate this."

*"Do these include serious illnesses?"*

"Yes, there doesn't appear to be any difference in how serious the illnesses were among the people who were healed and the people who were not healed or were only healed temporarily.

For example, someone who is HIV positive says that his HIV-level, which was right up at 151,000 before the meetings, came down to just 16,000 after the healing he believes he experienced. There are also people with cancer in this group of those apparently healed.

We have two kind of patients in this group: One with patients who can say that there sickness is gone now. But because of their long-time disease

170

*Majbrit Andersen has followed some of the people who were healed after their healing, and her study shows that it is taboo to talk about supernatural healing in the medical system.*

they still may have some symptoms, i.e. we have a cancer patient who had been in palliative chemotherapy treatment for terminal ovary cancer. The tumor in her ovary started to diminish in the meeting and after three months it disappeared (from being 4.3 cm in diameter) along with part of the scar tissue from an earlier operation. But the patient is still very tired.

We have another group who have had an essential improvement in their symptoms. The patients might actually be healed but we have no test that can prove it. I.e. we have a patient with sclerosis who was not able to walk before without a helper and a stick. Spontaneously she started to walk in the meeting and now she can walk stairs without any help for the first time in five and a half years.

Finally there is a fourth category containing five people, of which two are actually dead, and the three others haven't given sufficient information", says Majbrit Andersen.

## Does faith have an impact?

The questionnaires don't ask whether or not people are believing Christians. But Majbrit Andersen has the feeling that the response group is not predominantly made up of believing Christians. Many, for example, have commented that they have also used alternative healers and new age methods which people don't normally go for in Christian circles.

But Majbrit Andersen doesn't dare comment on whether the Christians were healed to a greater extent than the non-Christians.

"There are examples of both, but our studies don't investigate the Christian aspect. It's a purely medical study", says Majbrit Andersen.

171

## Doctors will not accept...

But the study also showed that many people feel shy about sharing their supernatural experiences with doctors. They felt that they were not taken seriously and that their doctors closed out any supernatural explanations – even when it was obvious that something extraordinary had happened.

Majbrit Andersen selected ten patients – typical for the different categories – and interviewed them. She was able to see their medical journals, but she ran into a problem: Most of the patients didn't want to involve their doctors. Some didn't even want to be tested after the healing. The reason might be that the "healed" patients were afraid the test would show that they hadn't actually been healed. Another reason might be that they didn't want to experience the hostile attitude of the biomedical "system" towards non-medical healing – such as spiritual healing in the name of Jesus.

Here are some examples from the report:

## It *must* be the chemotherapy...

BERIT was the one with a cancerous tumor in her ovary. In her own eyes and in the eyes of ordinary people she is totally healed. The tumor disappeared. Even scar tissue from an earlier operation is gone. Still the specialist in pathology who read and evaluated her journal is only looking for the reason in the chemotherapy that helped her in the first place (the cancer went into remission for three years), but didn't seem to help her during the last year, and even gave her serious side effects - until she turned up at Charles Ndifon's meetings in March 2001. In the journal it is even mentioned that the last chemotherapy treatment has just been given as palliative care – that means: No hope of healing. And that the patient, with the support of the hospital, received the highest disablement pension at short notice ...

In the end the specialist admits, "the signals from the oncologist have been so pessimistic that the patient of course has to interpret this as a miracle." No wonder! She was healed, and now she can do many things and she is happy again.

Berit tells how she was informed by a doctor at the beginning that she had cancer and should have six chemotherapy treatments. No compassion was shown according to Berit. It was just facts. It only took about ten minutes all together, and she was shocked. She was actually so affected that she fell off the chair! (It was a chair with wheels, and somehow she managed to fall off because she was sitting on the edge.) Finally the doctor, who was a woman, asked her: "Do you have any questions or are you just in shock?" And Berit couldn't think of anything, so she was left alone in the room - with something that looked like a death sentence.

Berit had six treatments with chemotherapy. These probably saved her from death initially. But after three years the cancer broke out again, and if it hadn't been for the Jesus-healing, she *would* probably be dead today…

## "This is not exceptional…"

ESTHER was checked both before and after the healing by a doctor who was at the meeting in Copenhagen. Charles Ndifon insisted on this. The doctor concluded before the healing that Esther had two tumors in her breast and three in the armpit. Big ones. After the healing the same doctor came again and checked Esther.

"She was looking perplexedly at my face and said: 'They are gone'. And she checked again and again both here and there, and she said: 'They are gone, but… yes they are gone'." The tumors in her armpit had disappeared. This was confirmed by the doctor afterwards. According to Esther, the tumors in her breast also disappeared for a long time, but recently she felt a new tumor in her breast. And unfortunately she didn't want to be scanned and tested at the hospital, so we cannot know if it is cancer or if she actually was healed – though it seems so.

After the healing Esther still had diarrhea, but after she had been prayed for again in another church that disappeared as well. Esther could start working again and was very active.

But what does the pathology specialist conclude after seeing her journal? That the reason might be that the patient stopped receiving hormonal treatment some time before, and that this case can not be described as totally exceptional…

## It's taboo for doctors

HELLE was apparently healed of disseminated sclerosis – she started to walk at the meeting within five minutes, and her situation has been better ever since. Before, she had to sit in a wheel chair or walk with the help of a stick and a helper. She was sent to a neurology hospital unit thirty three times during her five and a half years with sclerosis. Now she can run around and climb. She is twenty seven years old. She still suffered some small attacks in

173

the time after the meeting, but throughout all of 2002 she has had no attacks at all, and to any ordinary person she looks completely healed. But medically speaking she is not healed as long as she still has (had) attacks.

The psychiatry specialist explains her much better condition as resulting from the treatment with beta interferon and prednisolone. But she had already been on that treatment for nearly one year with no improvement when the "miracle" happened – and it happened in just one night – actually in five minutes.

When Helle told her doctor at the hospital that she had been healed, she sensed his attitude and said straight out, "Poul, I don't care what you think, but I know what happened that night. I experienced that miracle." The doctor's reaction was, that he quickly started to perform his usual test and Helle felt that he was suddenly very busy. But in the end he said, "I can see that you are much better now. And that's good." And he explained it partly by the medication …

Later Helle told her personal doctor and he is happy for her, that she is now feeling better.

She says: "I don't think you can normally feel so much better because of what happens in one night. But he can't talk about it either. It's taboo, you are not supposed to talk about it", Helle concludes.

## Overview

Below is an overview reproduced from the first summary statement. This is a working paper which we have been given permission to use. In some cases changes may have later taken place – for example in connection with new visits to healing meetings. In the first place, twenty nine people fell into category 1 – later two were added from category 2. One person was later added to the group of seventy five. This explains the differences between the numbers mentioned. But this gives a very good overview of what happened to the people looking for healing. Explanations have been added in brackets for some of the medical expressions.

## Category 1: Still healed after 6 months
### 29 (now 31) out of 75 indicated that they still feel they are healed.

1. Multiple sclerosis patient has experienced significant improvement in mobility. Was previously supported by a walking stick and helper, now walks without assistance.

2. Tumor in a lymph gland on the neck is gone.

3. Patient receiving palliative chemotherapy after curative treatment abandoned. After Ndifon meeting, the tumor in her ovary disappeared (from being 4.3 cm in diameter) along with part of the scar tissue from an earlier operation.

4. Congenital blindness in right eye changed to ability to distinguish light and dark. (about 10% vision)

5. Pain in back for 14 days due to wrenching, disappeared.

6. HIV-patient's HIV blood level of 151,000/ml fell by 90% to 16,000/ml.

7. Patient with nerve inflammation (wheelchair user) with no sensitivity in LE (= the legs) for three years, experienced burning sensation in her feet. Mobility has since improved to the point where she can walk 600-700 meters. Patella reflex (= knee reflex) is also intact again.

8. Patient with breast cancer with liver metastasis (= spreading from a cancer in the liver) had much better liver count.

9. Diabetes patient (type 2) with a normal BS (= blood sugar level) of about 12, now has BS of 5-6.

10. Back pain disappeared, leading to increased mobility.

11. A friend's cancer disappeared?

12. Depression, migraine disappeared.

13. Lump in breast disappeared. Cancer?

14. Whiplash suffered for two and a half years has disappeared.

15. Dissolution of liver metastasis (= spreading from a cancer, new cancer tumors) demonstrated by a scan.

16. Multiple sclerosis over fifteen years. Patient has attained a positive improvement, physically/mentally.

17. Whiplash requiring daily intake of 10-12 aspirin/codeine tablets at times - now has much less of a headache and takes about 2 tablets per week.

18. Knee pain over five years making it impossible for patient to run, completely disappeared.

19. Patient can bend a finger which used to be stiff, but with some muscle tension.

20. Patient with several eye problems and resultant blurry vision experienced momentary clear vision during the meetings. Began medical treatment 2-3 days afterwards.

21. Pain associated with kidney stone disappeared. Kidney stone gone?

22. Ischias pain gone, ischemia (= insufficient blood supply) in the legs is

much improved.

23. Stomach pains over 2-3 months, heartburn, hemorrhoids disappeared.

24. Breast cancer with metastasis (= spreading from a cancer) to lymph nodes for the same armpit. All tumors are gone, along with diarrhea.

25. Whiplash and neck injury over six years due to assault. Taking max. daily intake of ibuprofen tablets about 3-4 times a week. Now has free movement, almost pain-free. Ibuprofen once a week.

26. Onychomycosis (= fungal nail infection) over 12 years, extremely dry, scaly skin on both lower legs for 25 years, is almost gone, significant improvement.

27. Sinus problems: improvement. Tinnitus over 3 years: improvement. Backache over 40 years: less tension.

28. Menieres disease (= episodic ear disease): no episodes since Ndifon. Back injury: top of the pain is gone, increased mobility. But has had one relapse.

29. Diabetes patient receiving medication (two Orabet tablets daily) completely stopped treatment due to a lasting fall in blood sugar levels. Now takes 1 tablet a day.

## Category 2: Temporarily healed

**28 (now 26) out of 75 say that they were well for a period of time, but have since become sick again.**

1.  Chronic back pain due to congenital lumbar lordosis: disappeared for four days.

2.  Asthma, ischemia (= lack of blood supply) in the legs: could manage stairs more easily for two weeks.

3.  Chronic retinitis pigmentosa (= an infection which causes black spots on the retina and thus disrupts the field of vision): gone for six months. After that, partial relapse.

4.  Pain due to degenerative arthritis in the hip disappeared for 1 week.

5.  Compulsive thoughts / anxiety significantly improved. But still come occasionally.

6.  Painful, growing, fatty tumors got smaller and were not painful during the meetings. Pain in the knees and hips also disappeared. Slowly returned to the previous bad state.

7.  Partial improvement to inflammation in the shoulders.

8.  Heart neurosis, arthritis in the groin and hip abated. Came back, but

less than before.

9. Whiplash: partial relapse.

10. Knee injury: short-term improvement. Leg shortened by 3 cm: lasting.

11. Same as 10 below.

12. Two children with a rare disease (not mentioned for the sake of anonymity) did not empty bowels in their nappies for a week, compared to several times a day normally.

13. General dystonia (= abnormal muscle contractions). Reduced in the stomach region, temporary improvement to foot position (crooked due to the dystonia).

14. Partial improvement of diabetes type 2 due to constant fall in daily BS (= blood sugar), from 2 to 1 Orabet tablets daily.

15. Pelvic pain over 8 years disappeared for 2 weeks.

16. Right eye watered constantly for 1 year. Stopped after the meetings, for six months.

17. Patient with lung cancer experienced easier breathing, less pain, but relapsed.

18. Damaged ear bone and resultant unilateral deafness: temporary improvement.

19. Right eye: blind. Left eye: 5% vision. Temp. improvement to vision.

20. Back pain due to a fall from scaffolding: slight improvement.

21. Whiplash pain disappeared for ½ an hour.

22. Brain tumor: fewer attacks, shorter duration.

23. Shoulder pain: disappeared for a few days.

24. Ear pain / tinnitus: disappeared for 5-6 days.

25. Deformed foot (30% disability): temporary improvement (better walking).

26. Gallstone attacks: fewer and shorter attacks – but declining.

27. Lumbar problems—pain and fatigue: disappeared for 1 week.

28. Arthritis in shoulder: the pain disappeared for 5 ½ months.

29. Nervous condition: big improvement lasting 1 week.

30. Partial improvement to tinnitus, fewer attacks.

## Category 3: Not healed after all

**13 out of the 75 now say - 6 months afterwards – that they weren't actually healed after all.**

1. Arthritis: unchanged.

2. Multiple sclerosis: unchanged.
3. Asthma: unchanged.
4. Problems with stomach acid: unchanged.
5. Broken shin: unchanged. Psychological improvement.
6. Digestion difficulties: unchanged.
7. Arthritis in hip and fingers: unchanged.
8. Multiple sclerosis: unchanged, although some violent spasms disappeared.
9. Slipped disk: unchanged.
10. Tinnitus: unchanged.
11. Arthritis: unchanged.
12. Diabetes: unchanged.
13. Was in the process of receiving treatment for breast cancer. Experienced psychological improvement for two weeks.

## Category 4: Incomplete data / dead.

**3 patients gave such incomplete information that they have not been included.**

**2 had died within the 6 month period.**

1. ALS (= Leukemia) patient died.
2. Patient with testicular and abdominal cancer: for three months after the meetings, the tumor marker had fallen from 28,000 (AFP) to 9,000, and the lump had gotten smaller despite chemotherapy having been abandoned due to lack of effect. The patient died recently.

Notes:

1 On 24 October 1999, William Harris published a study, in *Archives of Internal Medicine* , into the effects of prayer in a trial involving over 1000 heart patients at Saint Luke's Hospital in Kansas, USA. The study indicates a positive effect of prayer at a distance (without the patients being aware of it) in a controlled, double-blind, clinical trial. This and other studies will be discussed in a later chapter.

2 Pregraduate study: Physiological and psychological experiences with religious treatment - in relation to the patients comprehension of their illness and their experiences with the public health service. Med. stud. Majbrit Bruun Andersen, Almen Medicin, Institut for Sundhedstjenesteforskning. Det Sundhedsvidenskabelige Fakultet, Syddansk Universitet 2002.

# Scientific studies into the effects of prayer

**Since the dawn of time, prayer has been used as part of – or the only – treatment for illness. But the effects have only very recently been investigated scientifically.**

Modern medical science has specialized one-sidedly in combating illness based on a materialistic[1] worldview – without the spiritual dimension. And also without a God who hears prayer.

But even our highly developed medical science is, of course, unable to heal all illnesses. And the one-sided emphasis on the biological and chemical side of treatment has given rise to a jungle of alternative "spiritual" treatment methods, which generally lie outside what is recognized by the public health system. Many of these "techniques" have doubtful effects, and the occult links to Eastern religions ought to perhaps be of concern to the users. If you make use of spiritual forces, you are taking a big risk. You suddenly find yourself in a world in which both positive and destructive forces exist. Many discover too late that they have hitched their horse to the wrong wagon in order to escape their illness...

As a result, over the last few decades, renewed interest has arisen in the – often forgotten – spiritual dimensions of the Christian faith. And here it's chiefly the power of prayer which some researchers have decided to investigate – purely scientifically.

## Byrd's trial: Intercession works

In 1988, R. C. Byrd published a study into *"Positive therapeutic effects of intercessory prayer in a coronary care unit population"*.

It was published in the scientific American journal, *South Medical Journal.*[2]

The study involved 393 patients in the cardiac ward at San Francisco General Hospital in California.

The trial was controlled. Randomly selected patients either received normal treatment without organized prayer, or were included in the experiment, whereby patients, without their knowledge, received prayer by people outside the hospital, whom they didn't know.

However, for ethical reasons, the patients in this trial were asked beforehand whether they would participate in the trial. fifty seven of the four hundred and fifty patients (12 per cent) refused to participate for religious or personal reasons. The remainder participated, and knew about the trial, but didn't know which group they had been allocated to. The disadvantage (or advantage?) of this trial was that the patients who received prayer were thus "receptive" – while those who didn't receive intercession were also made aware of the possibility of intercession.

The staff were also informed about the trial. But they didn't know which patients where prayed for and which were not. The people praying were given information about the diagnosis, general health and any changes in the condition of the people they were praying for.

Byrd and his colleagues found that the patients in the prayer group had fewer strokes, less need for diuretic treatment or antibiotics, had fewer cases of pneumonia, had fewer cardiac arrests and had less requirements for IV drip and oxygen than the other patients.

But from a statistical viewpoint, they had the problem that there was only evidence of a so-called "significant" difference in six cases.

But Byrd's study showed that the patients in the intercession group had a significantly better outcome (statistically), if one measured their condition using a measuring scale, called CCU, which was already used at the hospital. However, the length of time that the patients stayed in the cardiac ward was no different between the two groups.

## Other trials: No measurable result

Another experiment carried out by O'Lahoire was published in 1997[3]. It was aimed at investigating the effect of prayer/healing on psychological problems such as self-esteem, anxiety and depression.

406 patients took part in the trial and were divided into three groups, either with no prayer, direct prayer or indirect prayer from the 90 healers/prayers.

But the trial failed to demonstrate specific results from the intercession beyond what might have been the result of a placebo effect – i.e. where the patient improves because he *believes* in the treatment – just like if you give the patient a sugar tablet with no effects.

Another smaller pilot study by S.R. Walker et. al, 1997[4], in which they investigated the effects of intercession on forty alcoholics during treatment, also failed to demonstrate any *measurable* effect.

## Long-term trial of healing AIDS patients at a distance

F. Sicher[5] et al chose forty AIDS patients in the advanced stages of the disease for their trial (via advertisements and contacts with the homosexual environment), to participate in a six month trial of the value of healing at a distance. The trial thus involved relatively few patients but on the other hand, any changes were measured over a six month period. All the patients were aware of the project, but didn't know if they themselves had been subject to healing at a distance. Half of the forty were not.

The experiment was double-blind, in that neither the patients or the doctors who were treating them knew which patients where subject to healing at a distance. The patients were also matched so that the twenty in the healing group and the twenty in the control group were as similar as possible in terms of gender, age, etc. Prior to the experiment, the health of the patients was also tested thoroughly.

In all, forty "healers" took part. They came from Christian, Jewish, Buddhist, native American or Shaman traditions, while some had trained in bioenergy and meditation. And there is no information about which types of healers had the best results.

In order to be able to participate, the healers had to have been practicing for at least five years, and have experience in the remote healing of at least ten patients, as well as experience with healing AIDS patients. The healers selected had an average of seventeen years' experience and 106 remote patients. After six months, the patients in the healing group had:

1) Significantly fewer AIDS related illnesses
2) A less serious level of illness
3) Significantly fewer visits to their doctor
4) Significantly fewer days spent in hospital
5) Significantly better general condition than those in the control group.

The entire group – including those who didn't receive healing at a distance – generally experienced improvement initially, which the study ascribes to the fact that they gained hope and the expectation that something was at last going to happen with their incurable disease. In contrast to the other trials investigating the effect of Christian intercession, the healers here could also make use of their religious remedies and instruments.

## Large trial involving over 1,000 patients

In 1999, Dr. William S. Harris, et al, published a large study[6] which demonstrated a significant positive effect from remote intercession (in this case Christian intercession). This study is currently seen as the biggest and most reliable investigation which has been carried out into the effect of prayer on the sick.

In contrast to the AIDS study, these heart patients knew nothing about the study. Not even the staff knew anything about the trial (unlike Byrd's trial), which meant that there weren't only "receptive" patients in the intercession group, and neither patients nor staff could influence the result.

The study followed up on Byrd's trial from 1988.

The goal was to investigate whether the hypothesis which could be derived from Byrd's results, could be proven, i.e.: That patients who – without being aware of it – are prayed for by intercessors at another location and who don't know them, will experience fewer complications and will have shorter hospital stays than patients who don't receive the same intercession.

## Who were the intercessors?

The intercessors weren't special healers, as in some of the other trials, but were randomly selected from the local environment among Christian people who believed that prayer has an effect. They did not have to come from particular Christian traditions. The largest group (35 per cent) professed to be non-denominational (i.e. Christians who didn't belong to a specific church tradition), 27 per cent were Episcopalians (the American version of the English Anglican church), while the remainder belonged to various protestant or catholic groups.

They all had this in common: they had to be able to accept this statement:

*"I believe in God. I believe he is personal[7] and is interested in the lives of individuals. I also believe that he reacts to prayers for healing which are prayed on behalf of the sick."*

The majority of the intercessors (87 per cent) were women, with an average age of 56. All of them went to church (at least) once a week, and prayed each day – even before the trial. All of the intercessors had started praying within one and a half days of receiving notification about their prayer subjects.

## The patients knew nothing

The trial took place at the Mid America Heart Institute, Saint Luke's Hospital, Kansas City, USA and was carried out in cooperation with the University of Missouri (Division of Cardiology, Dept. of Medicine) in Kansas and the University of California (Dept. of Preventive Medicine) in San Diego.

A total of 1,019 patients were admitted to the Saint Luke's Hospital cardiac ward during the trial period. 6 patients were excluded for practical reasons, since they had to receive heart transplants. The remaining 1,013 patients were randomly allocated to two groups:

529 patients (52 %) in the group which received normal treatment without intercession, and

484 patients (48 %) in the group which received normal treatment with intercession.

The difference in the numbers was due to matters of chance.

Patients who ended up being admitted for less than 24 hours were removed from the study.

The 529 who didn't receive prayer was thus reduced to 524 patients (minus 5), and

The 484 who received prayer was reduced to 466 patients (minus 18).

The patients in both groups had an average age of 66 years, and were fairly evenly divided between men and women (66 % and 61 % in the intercession and non-intercession groups, respectively).

## The staff knew nothing

Just as the patients knew nothing about the trial, neither did the staff know about the two groups. In fact, they didn't even know that a study was being carried out. The trial was thus completely blind, with no person or factor being able to influence the result – apart from the intercession. Not even the intercessors knew more about the patients than their first names.

## The results of the study

In order to compare the results, a points system was used, MAHI-CCU[8], where 1 indicates the lowest degree of illness and 6 indicates death.

1 point = heart fibrillation, need for antibiotics, etc.[9]

2 points = need for IV drip, heart medication, development of pneumonia,[10]

3 points = need for temporary pacemaker or smaller operation[11]

4 points = need for permanent pacemaker or other serious operation[12]

5 points = cardiac arrest[13]

6 points = death[14]

MAHI-CCU contains all the illness elements a patient might be expected to have while suffering from heart disease.

If one didn't take into account differences in the seriousness of the illness elements, but simply added up how many illness elements were found in the patients, it was found that there were 10 per cent fewer illness elements among the patient group which received intercession than in the other group.

After this, a "weighted" count was used, whereby a mild illness element in group 1 gave 1 point, while a more serious element from group three gave 3 points, etc. Thus the most serious conditions gave the most points.

A patient can also easily pass through several levels during their stay, and if the patient had several of the conditions mentioned, he or she accumulated the corresponding number of points.

When the number of points were thus counted based on the degree of seriousness of the illness elements, the result was that there were 11 per cent fewer points scored in the intercession group than in the other group.

*In general, the patients in the intercession group had a lower score in all fields which related to negative development in their illness.*

## Prayer and patient contribution?

As an experiment, they then tried to use the same model for measuring patient condition as Byrd had used in his trial. Byrd only used three divisions for the patient's condition: Good, Medium and Bad. Based on this less precise measurement, the difference between the intercession group and the other group was not significant – even though there was a difference. In other words, a more precise weighting was required in order to see the difference in Harris' study. The results (in per cent) were distributed as follows:

| Condition | Control group | Intercession group | Difference |
|-----------|---------------|--------------------|-----------| 
| **Good** | 64.5 % | 67.4 % | + 2.9 % |
| **Medium** | 71 % | 63 % | - 8 % |
| **Bad** | 115 % | 89 % | - 26 % |

Given that Byrd, et al, had still found a significant effect in their *own* study, could this perhaps be because the patients themselves were aware of the intercession and thus *contributed*? – that they believed in/counted on the possible effect of prayer?

In Harris' study, the patients didn't know that they were being prayed for.

## Same period of time in hospital

A significantly shorter length of stay was not observed for the intercession patients in Dr. Harris' study. But the average in both groups was also just four days – counted from the day after admission, which is when intercession began. Two patients in the intercession group had stays of 137 and 161 days – which was twice as long as any of the other patients in the whole trial. But even if these were removed from the calculations, there was still no significant difference.

## Supplementary prayer

Dr. Harris concludes in his article in the *Archives of Internal Medicine*, that "when one evaluates the results of this investigation, it is important to note that we are presumably studying the effect of *supplementary* intercession. Given that at least fifty per cent of the patients indicated to the hospital that they had a religious preference, it is likely that many – if not the majority – of patients in both groups *already* received intercession and/or direct prayer from friends and family or ministers during their admission."[15]

## What is the explanation?

Dr. Harris refers to two books which deal with the subject, "How prayer heals"[16] and "Why patients use alternative medicine"[17]. These authors have attempted to find both natural and supernatural explanations for the positive "mechanism" which clearly comes into effect when the sick are prayed for.

Those who lean towards a "natural explanation" believe that the positive effect of prayer is real enough, but is an as yet unknown physical force which is set in motion by the intercessor and received by the person being prayed for. The supernatural explanations fall outside of the domain of science, and Harris doesn't comment any further on these:

"The goal of this study was not to investigate a mechanism, but a phenomenon. Clearly the evidence for the phenomenon has to precede any explanation of it."

Harris also claims that the goal wasn't to prove God's existence:

"We can simply demonstrate that when a person outside the hospital says or thinks the first name of a patient at the hospital, in an attitude of intercession, that patient apparently gains a better cardiac ward experience."

## Conscious faith and prayer are beneficial

That a patient's *own* spiritual orientation or religious faith also has an impact on their health is more obvious. This has already been shown many times.

Two recent American books, *"The Faith Factor"*[18] and *"Is Religion Good for Your Health?"*[19] have shown that there is a connection between church membership/going to church and a better state of health. This is also borne out by a number of statistical studies[20].

People who believe in God and pray during their illness appear to have better health and a better recovery than people who don't believe and pray. For example, T. E. Oxman, et al, have studied the risk factors associated with death after a heart operation and have shown that the social relationships, and the strength and comfort which religion can give people reduces their risk[21].

H.G Koenig, et al, have shown that elderly male hospital patients were better at avoiding depression if they were religious.[22] Koenig has also shown a positive effect on blood pressure in the aged as a result of their religious activity.[23]

J. A. Blumenthal, et al, have shown that faith is effective in combating stress and can reduce the risk of dying from a heart attack.[24]

However, the idea that people's religious beliefs can have a positive effect on their state of health is really not that unthinkable. It's fairly obvious that the comfort and strength one gains in difficult situations from having "God in control" must have a positive effect – at the very least a psychological one. But there are also studies which suggest that faith affects our hormones and our immune system.[25]

## Large German study of 35,000 people: Faith is healthy

Having a living faith has great significance for one's health and well-being. This has been confirmed by Professor Ronald Grosarth-Maticek, leader of the department for preventative medicine at "The European Center for Peace and Development", in Heidelberg.

The German professor sent out questionnaires to 35,000 people in Germany, from which it was apparent that faith is the single factor which has the *greatest significance* for good health.

The other factors were:
- *physical:* ailments, diet, exercise, sleep

- *mental:* enthusiasm, possibility to do activities, self determination
- *social:* good relationships, good integration.

Many of the responses to the investigation went something like this, "Thanks to my personal contact with God, I always feel a healing effect in my body and soul", or, "God has led me all my life, protected and loved me".

Vilfred Veeser from the "Training Initiative for Preventative Pastoral Care and Counseling" believes that the reason for the positive results is that Christians can unburden their sorrows and confide in God.

"It helps them to live more consciously in the moment. A Christian also lives a more relaxed life because he knows that this life is not all there is. And relaxation strengthens the immune system." [26]

(At the same time, it must also be conceded that faith – at least according to one study[27] – can apparently lead to greater mortality in the aged, who suffer under internal religious struggles).

The interesting thing about the studies which Dr. Harris, et al, carried out was that intercession for a person by others apparently had a positive effect – even though the patients were completely unaware that they were being prayed for. No other study had yet shown that.

Notes:
1 That there is nothing in existence over and above matter and matter in motion.
2 South Med. J. 1988;81:826-829
3 O'Lahoire, S. An experimental study of the effects of distant, intercessory prayer on self-esteem, anxiety, and depression. Altern Ther Health Med. 1997; 3:38-53.
4 Walker SR, Tonigan Js, Miller WR, Corners, Kahlich L: Intercessory prayer in the treatment of alcohol abuse and dependence: a pilot investigation. Altern Ther Health Med. November 1997; 3:79-86.
5 *A Randomized Double-Blind Study of the Effect of Distant Healing in a Population with Advanced AIDS.* Sicher, F., Targ, E., Moore, D., & Smith, H.S. Western Journal of Medicine. 169: 356-363, 1998.
6 William S. Harris, Ph.D. A Randomized, Controlled Trial of the Effects of Remote, Intercessory Prayer on Outcomes in Patients Admitted to the Coronary Care Unit. Archives of Internal Medicine 1999;159:2273-2278.
7 By defining God as *personal*, the trial distanced itself from the new age perception of "god" as an impersonal power or "energy".
8 Mid America Heart Institute-Cardiac Care Unit (MAHI-CCU) Scoring System
9 (1) Need for antianginal agents, antibiotics, arterial monitoring, or catheterization; development of unstable angina
10 (2) Need for antiarrhythmic, inotropic, diuretic, or vasodilator drugs; development of pneumonia, atrial fibrillation supraventricular tachycardia, hypotension, or anemia, requiring a transfusion

11 (3) Need for a temporary pacemaker, Swan-Ganz catheterization, an implanted cardiac defibrillator; an electrophysiology study, radiofrequency ablation, or an interventional coronary procedure (ie, a percutaneous transluminal coronary angioplasty); development of third-degree heart block, extension of infarct, or gastrointestinal bleed; or readmission to the cardiac care unit

12 (4) Need for a permanent pacemaker, an intra-aortic balloon pump, major surgery (of any kind), percutaneous transluminal coronary angioplasty with stent placement and/or rotablator or intubation/ventilation; development of congestive heart failure, ventricular tachycardia, ventricular fibrillation, or sepsis

13 (5) Cardiac arrest

14 (6) Death

15 page 2277, column 1, Arch Intern Med/vol 159, Oct. 25, 1999.

16 Levin J. *How prayer heals: a theoretical model.* Altern Ther Health Med. January 1996;2:66-73.

17 Astin JA *Why patients use alternative medicine: results of a national study* JAMA 1998;279:1546-1553.

18 Manhews DA, Clark C. The Faith Factor - *Proof of the Healing Power of Prayer.* New York, NY, Penguin Group, 1998

19 Koenig HG. *Is Religion Good for Your Health?* Binghamton, NY: Haworth Press;1997.

20 Comstock GW, Partridge KB. *Church attendance and health. J Chronic Dis.* 1972; 25:665-672

Gardner JW, Lyon JL. *Cancer in Utah Mormon women by church activity level.* Am J Epidemiol. 1977;116:258-265.

Graham TW, Kaplan BH, Cornoni-Huntley JC, et al. *Frequency of church attendance and blood pressure elevation.* J behav Med. 1978;1:37-43.

21 Oxman TE, Freeman OH Jr. Manheimer ED Lack of social participation or religious strength and comfort as risk factors for death after cardiac surgery in the elderly. *Psychosom Med.* 1995;57:5-15.

22 Koenig HG, Cohen HJ, Blazer DC, et al. Religious coping and depression among elderly hospitalized medically ill men. *Am J Public Health.* 1992;149:1693-1700.

23 Koenig HG, George LK, HaysJC, Larson DB, Cohen HJ Slazer DG. *The relationship between religious activities and blood pressure in older adults* Int J Psychiatry Med. 1998;28:189-213.

24 Blumenthal JA Jiang W, Babyak MA, et al. *Stress management and exercise training in cardiac patients with myocardial ischemia: effects on prognosis and evaluation of mechanisms.* Arch Intern Med. 1997;157:2213-2223

25 Kiecoit-Glaser JK, Garner W, Speicher CE, Penn G, Glaser R: *Psychosocial modifiers of immunocompetence in medical students.* Psychosom Med. 1984:46:7-14.

Selye H. *The Stress of Life.* New York, NY: McGraw-Hill, 1956.

26 According to the German news organization, Idea Spektrum.

27Kenneth I. Pargament, PhD; Harold G. Koenig, MD; Nalini Tarakeshwar, MA; June Hahn, PhD *Religious Struggle as a Predictor of Mortality Among Medically Ill Elderly Patients A 2-Year Longitudinal Study.* Department of Psychology, Bowling Green State University, Bowling Green, OH 43403

# There has to be faith

Luther's showdown with Catholicism 500 years ago still makes it hard to speak openly about faith in many Protestant churches.

Does divine healing have anything to do with faith? "Yes, of course", most people would no doubt answer. And it does. That's clear from the New Testament as we shall see later. But among "orthodox" Christians there is a paradoxical doubt about the meaning of faith.

Strangely enough, it's often found to be harder for people who have been believing Christians for many years to receive healing. Intellectual theologians often have the same problem. And according to Charles Ndifon, it's related to the fact that *believing* Christians have gotten used to only believing *in theory*, and not in practice.

We will be looking specifically at this problem in this chapter, and the chapter is thus most relevant for people who have been conscious of their faith and believing Christians for many years. But the Bible references at the end of the chapter might be useful to all readers.

## Luther's showdown 500 years ago

How can it be that *faith* has become a problem among *believers* themselves?

There is no way around having to look at the history of the Lutheran church and the marks it has left – also in the other protestant denominations.

Martin Luther, as is well-known, had to have a big showdown with the wrong teachings and practices which had developed in the Catholic church of the time – over 500 years ago.

The Catholic church had been sidetracked, with concerns for the "church's" power and honor playing a greater role than the individual's simple faith.

The crudest example was that in order to gather money for St. Peter's church in Rome, the Pope had permitted the sale of so-called "indulgences". It's possible that the Pope originally had a pious motive with this, but in

189

practice, in any case, it ended up that dubious indulgence peddlers sold people forgiveness for their sins.

## The gift is free

Even the most unscrupulous villains could just *pay* their way out of their sins. And Luther, as an honest Christian, naturally had to react against this. As far as he could read in the New Testament, people could neither pay nor earn their way to the forgiveness of sins or eternal salvation. It was God who had given a gift in terms of what Jesus had done in taking the sins of the whole world upon himself and dying for it. And this gift from God was free – using the Bible's expression, it was: grace. And what you get by grace you shouldn't pay for, but you should just receive it and say thank you.

The Catholic church today does not disagree with this simple Christian message about "justification by faith". Theological discussions have been held at high levels for several years, and representatives from the Lutheran World Federation (LWF) and the Vatican, the leadership of the Catholic church, are now virtually as close to agreement on this 500 year old problem as is possible. A so-called *Joint Declaration on the Doctrine of Justification* was signed on 31 October 1999 on the actual Reformation day, which is also All Saints Day in Augsburg in Germany, where Luther broke with the Catholic church in 1530. The declaration declares, in brief, that we are saved by faith, but that good works are the sign that we are saved. Luther would also have been able to agree to that.

## Fear of "good works"

The Catholic church has thus moved on since 1530!

On the other hand, many modern Lutherans still apparently have trouble understanding that *faith* is not just an *intellectual* understanding of the fact that "God forgives everything" – but that the faith which is spoken about in the New Testament is an active faith – that it is a LIFE of faith and following Jesus. As you are no doubt aware, he didn't just say "believe!", but also, "Follow me!"[1] and "Sin no more!"[2]

*Jesus Christ thus called us to a new way of living.*

It's true that any good works we do can't earn us eternal salvation. Luther tried it himself, as a deeply serious Catholic monk, but he had to honestly admit that he failed.

But by reading the Bible himself – not just blindly accepting the

*Luther's showdown with Catholicism 500 years ago still makes it hard to speak openly about faith in many Protestant churches.*

interpretations of others – he discovered that God's grace is free and unconditional.

Only once this side of the matter is in place can we begin to do good. Because now we no longer do it to benefit ourselves (in order to be saved) but because we ARE saved. As John wrote, "We love, because he first loved us."[3]

This is a magnificent, liberating message, and we are indebted to Luther, that he rediscovered it and bravely held onto it when the great Roman world church had gone off track.

## Extreme Lutheranism?

But this magnificent message has unfortunately been quite distorted through the ages – in Luther's name.

Especially in very consciously *Lutheran* circles, people actually make a virtue out of the fact that one can and should *do* NOTHING. You just have to believe. And they are so afraid of "works Christianity" that even faith certainly mustn't become a performance, for otherwise it would also be something you *do*… Thus they even play down the meaning of faith. All that's left is baptism. And in the Lutheran church it's infant baptism. Because God has done everything, and we don't have to do anything. So eventually we might not even have to believe…?

This "extreme-Lutheran" attitude to faith has very little to do with original Lutheranism, as anyone can confirm by reading Luther's works. For example, if one just takes his Shorter Catechism,[4] there is much written about what we should do in order to preserve the faith in ourselves and our families. For Luther, faith was not just theory but practice – to believe is to live in faith.

But even if Luther did happen to say something which could be interpreted in this direction, as some believe, it falls to the ground in any case if Jesus in the New Testament said something else. And even if Popes and big personalities say something otherwise, it can never be more significant than what Jesus has said. After all, Luther, Augustine, Calvin, Zwingli, Wesley, Finney, Moody and all the other masters are just *interpreters* of the original: Jesus' teachings as we know them from the New Testament – the best attested ancient writings that exist.[5] What Jesus has said must always have first priority for genuine Christianity.

## Faith without faith…?

Today, Luther's teaching on "faith without works" is actually used to argue that not even *faith* is important.

In step with the trend of there being less faith *in practice*, some people have even made it a virtue to talk about how little faith they have.[7] We have become "proud of doubt, embarrassed about faith". It's fashionable to not trust anything or anyone, but to doubt everything. But that's *not* Christianity.

We need to go back to the starting point here, just as we do in all other areas of Christianity, where centuries of theological debate and hair-splitting – or lack of consistency – have muddied the simple message.

The New Testament is the closest we can get to original Christianity. It speaks unequivocally about faith being critical, as can be seen in the references below. Faith is mentioned several hundred times in the New Testament. And it is not least Jesus himself who teaches about faith's critical importance.

## Faith in connection with healings

Below are some examples of healings in the Bible. For almost every healing, something about faith is mentioned. No one, after reading these references, can be left in any doubt that faith has *critical* importance for healings – whether it be the sick person's own faith – or those who help them – or the person praying for the sick.

All three possibilities are mentioned in these references. And the critical thing is apparently not *who* has faith, but just that faith is present. Nor is it just a general faith in healing energy or psychological forces, but in every single case, a specific faith in the fact that Jesus Christ can heal.

# Read for yourself!

## The significance of faith for healing in the New Testament

In order to provide a simple overview, the whole account has not been quoted in each case, but by looking up the references in the New Testament you can easily find each section and read it all in context. Above each quote, a central phrase about the significance of faith for healing has been highlighted:

### Because you have so little faith...

¹⁴When they came to the crowd, a man approached Jesus and knelt before him. ¹⁵"Lord, have mercy on my son," he said. "He has seizures and is suffering greatly. He often falls into the fire or into the water. ¹⁶I brought him to your disciples, but they could not heal him."

¹⁷"O unbelieving and perverse generation," Jesus replied, "how long shall I stay with you? How long shall I put up with you? Bring the boy here to me." ¹⁸Jesus rebuked the demon, and it came out of the boy, and he was healed from that moment.

¹⁹Then the disciples came to Jesus in private and asked, "Why couldn't we drive it out?"

²⁰He replied, "Because you have so little faith. I tell you the truth, **if you have faith as small as a mustard seed**, you can say to this mountain, 'Move from here to there' and it will move. Nothing will be impossible for you."

(Matthew 17:14-20)

### "Go! It will be done just as you believed it would."

⁵When Jesus had entered Capernaum, a centurion came to him, asking for help. ⁶"Lord," he said, "my servant lies at home paralyzed and in terrible suffering."

⁷Jesus said to him, "I will go and heal him."

⁸The centurion replied, "Lord, I do not deserve to have you come under

my roof. But just say the word, and my servant will be healed. [9]For I myself am a man under authority, with soldiers under me. I tell this one, 'Go,' and he goes; and that one, 'Come,' and he comes. I say to my servant, 'Do this,' and he does it." [10]When Jesus heard this, he was astonished and said to those following him, "I tell you the truth, **I have not found anyone in Israel with such great faith.** [11]I say to you that many will come from the east and the west, and will take their places at the feast with Abraham, Isaac and Jacob in the kingdom of heaven. [12]But the subjects of the kingdom will be thrown outside, into the darkness, where there will be weeping and gnashing of teeth." [13]Then Jesus said to the centurion, **"Go! It will be done just as you believed it would."** And his servant was healed at that very hour.

(Matthew 8:5-13, Luke 7)

## When Jesus saw their faith

[3]Some men came, bringing to him a paralytic, carried by four of them. [4]Since they could not get him to Jesus because of the crowd, they made an opening in the roof above Jesus and, after digging through it, lowered the mat the paralyzed man was lying on. [5]When **Jesus saw their faith**, he said to the paralytic, "Son, your sins are forgiven."…

[11]"I tell you, get up, take your mat and go home." [12]He got up, took his mat and walked out in full view of them all. This amazed everyone and they praised God, saying, "We have never seen anything like this!"

(Mark 2:3-5, 11-12, Luke 5:18-21)

## Your faith has healed you

[20]Just then a woman who had been subject to bleeding for twelve years came up behind him and touched the edge of his cloak. [21]She said to herself, "If I only touch his cloak, I will be healed."

[22]Jesus turned and saw her. "Take heart, daughter," he said, **"your faith has healed you."** And the woman was healed from that moment.

(Matthew 9:20-22)

## "According to your faith will it be done to you"

[28]When he had gone indoors, the blind men came to him, and he asked them, "Do you believe that I am able to do this?" "Yes, Lord," they replied. [29]Then he touched their eyes and said, **"According to your faith** will it be done to you"; [30]and their sight was restored. (Matthew 9:28-30)

## "Woman, you have great faith!"

²²A Canaanite woman from that vicinity came to him, crying out, "Lord, Son of David, have mercy on me! My daughter is suffering terribly from demon-possession."

²³Jesus did not answer a word. So his disciples came to him and urged him, "Send her away, for she keeps crying out after us."

²⁴He answered, "I was sent only to the lost sheep of Israel."

²⁵The woman came and knelt before him. "Lord, help me!" she said.

²⁶He replied, "It is not right to take the children's bread and toss it to their dogs."

²⁷"Yes, Lord," she said, "but even the dogs eat the crumbs that fall from their masters' table."

²⁸Then Jesus answered, "Woman, you have **great faith**! Your request is granted." And her daughter was healed from that very hour.

(Matthew 15:22-28)

## If you have faith and do not doubt...

²¹Jesus replied, "I tell you the truth, if you have faith and do not doubt, not only can you do what was done to the fig tree, but also you can say to this mountain, 'Go, throw yourself into the sea,' and it will be done. ²²**If you believe**, you will receive whatever you ask for in prayer."(Matthew 21:21-22)

## "Why are you so afraid? Do you still have no faith?"

³⁷A furious squall came up, and the waves broke over the boat, so that it was nearly swamped. ³⁸Jesus was in the stern, sleeping on a cushion. The disciples woke him and said to him, "Teacher, don't you care if we drown?"

³⁹He got up, rebuked the wind and said to the waves, "Quiet! Be still!" Then the wind died down and it was completely calm.

⁴⁰He said to his disciples, "Why are you so afraid? Do you still have **no faith**?" (Mark 4:37-40)

## "Don't be afraid; just believe."

²²...[Jairus] fell at his feet ²³and pleaded earnestly with him, "My little daughter is dying. Please come and put your hands on her so that she will be healed and live." ²⁴So Jesus went with him...

³⁵While Jesus was still speaking, some men came from the house of Jairus, the synagogue ruler. "Your daughter is dead," they said.

"Why bother the teacher any more?"

[36]Ignoring what they said, Jesus told the synagogue ruler, "Don't be afraid; **just believe**."

[37]He did not let anyone follow him except Peter, James and John the brother of James...

[41]After he put them all out, he took the child's father and mother and the disciples who were with him, and went in where the child was.

He took her by the hand and said to her, "Talitha koum!" (which means, "Little girl, I say to you, get up!").

[42]**Immediately** the girl stood up and walked around (she was twelve years old). (Mark 5:22-24, 35-37, 41-42)

## "Don't be afraid; just believe, *and she will be healed.*"

[49]While Jesus was still speaking, someone came from the house of Jairus, the synagogue ruler. "Your daughter is dead," he said. "Don't bother the teacher any more." [50]Hearing this, Jesus said to Jairus, "Don't be afraid; **just believe**, and she will be healed." (According to Luke 8:49-50)

## "Receive your sight; your faith has healed you."

...but he shouted all the more, "Son of David, have mercy on me!"

[40]Jesus stopped and ordered the man to be brought to him. When he came near, Jesus asked him, [41]"What do you want me to do for you?"

"Lord, I want to see," he replied.

[42]Jesus said to him, "Receive your sight; **your faith** has healed you." [43]Immediately he received his sight and followed Jesus, praising God. When all the people saw it, they also praised God.

(Luke 18:39-43, Mark 10:51-52)

## Have faith in God!

[22]"Have faith in God," Jesus answered. [23]"I tell you the truth, if anyone says to this mountain, 'Go, throw yourself into the sea,' and does not doubt in his heart but believes that what he says will happen, it will be done for him. [24]Therefore I tell you, **whatever** you ask for in prayer, **believe that you have received it**, and it will be yours. [25]And when you stand praying, if you hold anything against anyone, forgive him, so that your Father in heaven may forgive you your sins." (Mark 11:22-25)

# Faith in action

*BEFORE: An African woman from Zimbabwe with lame feet was carried to the meeting.*

*AFTER: She is healed in the name of Jesus and walks around with Charles Ndifon on the platform. Behind her to the right one can still see her blanket.*

## "Your faith has saved you; go in peace."

⁴⁴Then he turned toward the woman and said to Simon, "Do you see this woman? I came into your house. You did not give me any water for my feet, but she wet my feet with her tears and wiped them with her hair. ⁴⁵You did not give me a kiss, but this woman, from the time I entered, has not stopped kissing my feet. ⁴⁶You did not put oil on my head, but she has poured perfume on my feet. ⁴⁷Therefore, I tell you, her many sins have been forgiven—for she loved much. But he who has been forgiven little loves little."

⁴⁸Then Jesus said to her, "Your sins are forgiven."

⁴⁹The other guests began to say among themselves, "Who is this who even forgives sins?" ⁵⁰Jesus said to the woman, "**Your faith has saved you**; go in peace." (Luke 7:44-50)

## "Where is your faith?"

²⁴The disciples went and woke him, saying, "Master, Master, we're going to drown!" ²⁵He got up and rebuked the wind and the raging waters; the storm subsided, and all was calm. "**Where is your faith?**" he asked his disciples. (Luke 8:24-25)

## "If you have faith as small as a mustard seed…"

⁵The apostles said to the Lord, "Increase our faith!"

⁶He replied, "**If you have faith** as small as a mustard seed, you can say to this mulberry tree, 'Be uprooted and planted in the sea,' and it will obey you." (Luke 17:5-6)

## Your faith has made you well

¹²As he was going into a village, ten men who had leprosy met him. They stood at a distance ¹³and called out in a loud voice, "Jesus, Master, have pity on us!"

¹⁴When he saw them, he said, "Go, show yourselves to the priests." And as they went, they were cleansed.

¹⁵One of them, when he saw he was healed, came back, praising God in a loud voice. ¹⁶He threw himself at Jesus' feet and thanked him—and he was a Samaritan.

¹⁷Jesus asked, "Were not all ten cleansed? Where are the other nine? ¹⁸Was no one found to return and give praise to God except this foreigner?" ¹⁹Then he said to him, "Rise and go; **your faith has made you well**." (Luke 17:12-19)

## That your faith may not fail

[31]"Simon, Simon, Satan has asked to sift you as wheat. [32]But I have prayed for you, Simon, that your **faith** may not fail. And when you have turned back, strengthen your brothers." (Luke 22:31-32)

## Jesus' name and the faith that comes through him

[12]When Peter saw this, he said to them: "Men of Israel, why does this surprise you? Why do you stare at us as if by our own power or godliness we had made this man walk? ... [16]**By faith** in the name of Jesus, this man whom you see and know was made strong. It is Jesus' name and the faith that comes through him that has given this complete healing to him, as you can all see. (Acts 3:12,16)

## ...saw that he had faith to be healed

[8]In Lystra there sat a man crippled in his feet, who was lame from birth and had never walked. [9]He listened to Paul as he was speaking. Paul looked directly at him, **saw that he had faith** to be healed [10]and called out, "Stand up on your feet!" At that, the man jumped up and began to walk. (Acts 14:8-10)

## We may approach God

[12]In Him (Jesus) and through **faith in Him** we may approach God with freedom and confidence. (Ephesians 3:12)

## Faith is confidence

[1]Now **faith is being sure** of what we hope for and certain of what we do not see. (Hebrews 11:1) NB: all of chapter 11 in Hebrews is about faith and its meaning throughout all of biblical history.

## Impossible without faith

[6]And **without faith** it is impossible to please God, because anyone who comes to Him must believe that He exists and that He rewards those who earnestly seek Him. (Hebrews 11:6)

## The testing of your faith...

...[3]because you know that the **testing** of your faith develops perseverance. [4]Perseverance must finish its work so that you may be mature and complete, not lacking anything. (James 1:3-4)

## But when he asks, he must believe and not doubt

[5]If any of you lacks wisdom, he should ask God, who gives generously to all without finding fault, and it will be given to him. [6]But when he asks, **he must believe** and not doubt, because he who doubts is like a wave of the sea, blown and tossed by the wind. [7]That man should not think he will receive anything from the Lord; [8]he is a double-minded man, unstable in all he does. (James 1:5-8)

## Faith - and action

[14]What good is it, my brothers, if a man claims **to have faith but has no deeds**? Can such faith save him? [15]Suppose a brother or sister is without clothes and daily food. [16]If one of you says to him, "Go, I wish you well; keep warm and well fed," but does nothing about his physical needs, what good is it? [17]In the same way, faith by itself, if it is not accompanied by action, is dead. (James 2:14-17)

## Faith without deeds is useless

[20]You foolish man, do you want evidence that **faith without deeds is useless**? (James 2:20)

## Faith overcomes

[4]for everyone born of God overcomes the world. This is the victory that has overcome the world, even our **faith**. (1 John 5:4)

1 E.g. in Matthew 19:21
2 E.g. "See, you are well again. Stop sinning or something worse may happen to you." (John 5:14)
3 1 John 4:19
4 www.ucc.org/faith/small.htm
5 While other historic events/writings, such as, for example, "Caesar's Gallic War" only exist in 9 or 10 copies, there are about 5,000 Greek, 10,000 Latin and 9,300 other manuscripts of the New Testament, as well as 36,000 quotes from the early church fathers.
6 For example, in the 1990's, Bishop Lodberg Hvas conducted a case against Rector Feldbæk because he made demands for faith in connection with baptism. The minister was dismissed. The whole case is documented in the book, "Tro og dåb i landsretten" (Faith and baptism in the High Court), Doxa forlag.
7 For example, famous Tv-journalist and teologian Jakob Højlund said in an interview, "I am a faithless person. That's why I go to church. My faith can only last a week." (Udfordringen, no. 30/2002)

# Do I have enough faith?

### A sermon by Charles Ndifon on faith
### - and accounts of unbelievable miracles

"What is faith", asks Charles, and answers himself:
"Faith is expectation.
Faith is not saying: 'I hope...'
When I ask: 'Do you expect to be healed?', many answer: 'I hope so.'
That's how some people react.

But if I ask you: 'Are you a man?', do you answer: 'Yes, I hope so anyway.'
No, if you are a man you say 'yes'. And if you are a woman you say 'no'. You
are not in any doubt."

## Faith is easier than you think
"I sometimes hear people say: 'Perhaps I don't have enough faith.' But I
can assure you that faith is not your problem.
To believe is much easier than you think.
Faith comes... Faith comes from what is heard.
That's what the Bible says: "faith comes from hearing the message, and
the message is heard through the word of Christ." (Romans 10:17).
The Bible doesn't say that faith comes from shouting and screaming, or
praying and fasting. Some people will try anything in order to be healed. But
all their efforts won't help them. That kind of thing is just religiosity.
I sometimes hear people say: 'I'm fasting in order to get a miracle.' Then I
say to them: 'My friend, go out and eat – and believe God's word! Then I
believe God will give you a miracle whether or not you are fasting.'
Friends, listen up! Faith is very simply to expect that God will do what He
says He will do.
But in order to have that faith, we have to first know what God says."

## Relax! It's not a lottery...
"People come and they stand and hope that perhaps the blessing will

also *touch* them. But if they think like that, perhaps they haven't understood what it is that happens.

You can just come and *hear* what God has to say to you, and you might be healed *just by hearing*.

Some people think that it's a mystery. Yes, perhaps they think it is a kind of lottery. Perhaps they will be lucky, and God will pull out their number. But it has nothing to do with luck.

Everyone can receive healing, if they will just listen.

When people come to me, they are so preoccupied with their sickness. They try so hard to be healed. I often have to ask them to relax. It's much easier than they think.

They stand there with their eyes screwed up and say: 'Oh, Oh, I am trying to be healed.'

I say to them: 'You have been trying that for a long time, and it doesn't work, so stop doing it. The way of faith is much simpler. Just believe in God's word. And act on God's word.'"

## Don't have faith in the opinions of people

"But many people have no idea what God says. They go after what people say.

But it's no use believing if your faith is based on people's opinions. Be sure of that! It's not about what the church traditions say, but about *God's* word.

Because in some churches they say: 'We don't really believe that healings can happen in our time.' Don't believe that, because that's not what God says in his word. God says: 'I am *your* healer.'

When you hear that, you should just say: 'Thank you Lord, I believe it.' Say thank you for what you have heard. That's faith. It's that simple.

And then you say: 'OK, now I believe that You are my healer, heal me!' You don't need to struggle. You can smile while you're doing it."

## Read the Bible yourself

"I want to encourage you to read the Bible. If you don't have a Bible, then buy one. You have to know what God says.

I myself was raised in a very religious home. But I had no idea what God actually said, before I read the Bible myself. And then I began to experience miracles. That's why you have to read it *yourself*.

A lot of things I had heard were what *other people* said *about* God.

People talk a lot about God, but God is not what *people* say he is. God is what He himself says he is. Hallelujah for that!

You have to get to know Him yourself. You have to know His character. Hallelujah. He is worth knowing.

Amen!"

## The man without eyes

Charles Ndifon has seen the most incredible healings. Sometimes he talks about these healings – simply to create faith in his hearers:

"You shouldn't be afraid that God can't heal you. Your sickness is not harder for God to heal than any others. I have helped to bring the dead back to life again. So I know what God's power can accomplish", he says. And then he talks about, for example, the man in Nashville, USA.

## How big is possible, God?

"In Nashville there was a blind man who came to one of my meetings. He was more than just blind; because the doctors had removed both of the man's eyes. He had had diabetes, which had made him blind, and in the end they had to surgically remove both his eyes.

His wife had to lead him to the meeting.

He came because one of his friends had been healed. His friend had been a cripple for 10 years. And he had been healed the previous night.

Now he came along himself to my meeting, and this is what happened:

I was in the process of ministering to the sick who wanted to be healed. There were people everywhere. So I didn't notice that he and his wife came forward. When I got to them I asked: 'What do you want?'

He answered: 'I have had diabetes, and I want to be able to see again.'

And I saw that in his left eye socket he had an eyeball. But it was made of plastic. In the other eye socket there was nothing at all. It was flat. And when he took the plastic eyeball out, the other socket was empty too.

'And you want to see?' I asked him.

'Yes, yes', he answered. I like people who say it like that. He didn't say something like: 'Well, I don't have any eyes… so…'. No, he believed it was possible.

But in the quietness of my mind I thought: 'How big is possible, God?' And God answered me: 'How big do you think I am?' So I said to the man:

'It's easy enough, if God can raise a dead person, he can also give you new eyes.' (Yes, brighten up, because if this is possible, your sickness is nothing!)

I just touched the man and said: 'I command this diabetes to leave this man.' Than I said: 'You blind spirit, come out of these eyes!' And then I said: 'Now I command these eyes to see!'"

## No change…

"But his eyes still looked the same as they had all along, and I know that many had expected the story to end differently. They had expected that his eyeballs just popped out. And others had expected that nothing would happen. But to the man I said: 'My friend, see!'

He had no eyes, lots of people would have answered: 'But I don't have any eyes to see with.' But here is a secret: Don't argue, just try to do what you can't do.

So this man really tried to see. He looked around him. He actually did this for 2-3 long minutes, and he just saw nothing. But he didn't say: 'Oh well, I can't see anything, it didn't work on me after all'. No, the man was determined. He wasn't going to turn around, he would go all the way. He believed that God could give him eyes. So he kept looking around. He didn't give up after two minutes."

## I can begin to see light…

"I spoke with him and tried to investigate his sight with light and other things. And suddenly, inside his eye sockets, I saw two small black dots. And they began to grow. And the man suddenly exclaimed: 'I can begin to see something now… I can see light. I can see something there, and there…'

And I was surprised myself, so I asked: 'Can you really see something?' 'Yes, I can see!'

At our office we have pictures of the man pointing around at the things he can see. What a wonderful miracle. God's WORD created new eyes in that man. Hallelujah! I can tell of hundreds of wonderful accounts like this one. For example, a woman who had one leg and wanted to have one more. And I said: 'In Jesus' name, receive it!' She removed her artificial limb and suddenly a leg began to grow, and she saw it and fainted. And people stood around exclaiming: 'Look at that!' And I was amazed too. It was really a wonderful miracle. That evening, her leg grew a certain amount, and it kept growing until it was complete."

## Incredible miracles continue to happen around the world

If you think what Charles Ndifon said about the man's eyes sounds too unbelievable, we can supplement it with this information about similar, almost unbelievable, miracles:

In Niels Christian Hvidt's latest book, "Mirakler"[1], which has just been released in Denmark by Gyldendals publishing firm in February 2002, he talks about 15 well-documented miracles. One of these happened to the eyes of an Italian woman, Gemma de Georgis, in 1947. She was born blind in 1939, but received her sight during a visit to the local saint Padre Pio, and she can still see perfectly. The particularly incredible thing, however, is that she still has no pupils! But she can see perfectly, and wanders around as walking evidence that God can do anything.

The book is full of mind blowing accounts which should cause any atheist to reconsider God's existence.

## Woken from the dead

But it is not enough that miracles are happening everywhere in these times: In Nigeria, in December 2001, a resuscitation of the dead occurred! Daniel Ekechukwu, pastor in the *Power Chapel Evangelical Church* in Onitsha, Nigeria, died on 30 November when the brakes on his 20-year-old car failed. But his wife wouldn't bury him before the German-born missionary, Reinhard Bonnke, had held a meeting in the town on 2 December. She took the man's body along to the meeting in a coffin, and it was placed on a table in an adjacent room, while Bonnke preached and prayed for the sick – knowing nothing about the dead man. Suddenly the dead man's chest began to move. Someone had a video camera and filmed the miracle as it happened. At first the man was cold and stiff, but

*Daniel Ekechukwu from Onitsha in Nigeria with his own death-certificate. After 3 days he came back to life.*

205

*The death certificate from St. Eunice's Clinic, signed by Dr. Jossy Anuebunisa, in which he states that Daniel Ekechukwu died in a car accident at 11.30 p.m. on November 30th, 2001.*

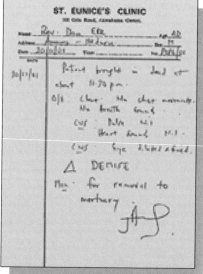

*The "dead" man beside his own coffin, and (right) happily reunited with his wife, Nneka, who didn't want to bury him.*

eventually warmth returned to his body again. The pastor could later tell people that he had seen both heaven and hell, and that he was to be the last warning to this generation about the seriousness of eternity.

Notes:
1 Niels Christian Hvidt: „Mirakler - møder mellem himmel og jord", page 116, Gyldendal, 2nd printing, 2002. Niels Chr. Hvidt is a Dane with a masters in theology, who teaches at the Gregoriana University in Rome.
2 The account can be seen at www.cfan.org/uk/testimonies/resurrection/page1.htm - where you can also order a video of the miracle. Bonnke spoke about the event himself in Benny Hinn's TV program on TNN and then on GOD Digital on Easter Thursday 2002. Later on he was on Pat Robertsons Club 700 on CBN.

# How can you hold onto your miracle...?

**Some people lose their healing after they have been healed. Can we do something ourselves to stay healthy?**

*"Does a person who has been healed have a responsibility themselves for preserving their miracle?"* we asked Ndifon.

"Let me ask you a simple counter question: Do you have a responsibility when you have been to your doctor?"

*"Um, yes…"*

"You might go to the doctor because you have a heart problem. You've been spending too much time at McDonalds and eaten too much junk food. And after a while your heart begins to react to what you're eating. You go to the hospital and the doctor says: 'You actually need an operation, but go home now and stop eating all that fatty food.'

When the doctor says this to you, do you just go back and continue living in an unhealthy way, as before?

No you don't, do you? But there are actually a lot of people who do.

Some people have cancer because they have smoked too much. They get healed. But no sooner are they well again than they go back and start smoking again.

Honestly, they might as well go out and shoot themselves. It's just common sense."

## There is a connection

"If you bang your head against a wall, and it hurts, you stop doing it, don't you? You don't bang your head against the wall again and expect that it won't hurt next time. It would be stupid, anyway, to expect that even though you do the same thing that the result would be different.

Things are connected. And that which gives you life is also that which keeps you alive. If Jesus heals you, then follow him! Then you will remain healthy. It's just common sense.

Several months ago, I got an email from a man in Denmark. His doctor had given him just a few weeks to live.

He had cancer in his throat, neck and back – all over his body he had cancer. And the doctor told him directly that the cancer was the result of his smoking. It's not something I made up, they were the doctor's words. I just told the man: Come to one of my meetings!

I preached, he believed, he received Jesus, and do you know what happened? He was completely healed. He went back to the doctor and he was in perfect health. The cancer had disappeared.

But then this man began to smoke again. And four months later I got a new email: The cancer had returned. After he had been healed, he stopped following Jesus. He just sat down and began to smoke again.

My friend, God doesn't heal you in order for you to serve the devil even better. He heals you in order to set you free. Free to live for him.

We have to see things in their right perspective."

## God wants you to be well

"In 3 John 1:2, John writes: 'Dear friend, I pray that you may enjoy good health and that all may go well with you, even as your soul is getting along well.'

Everyone wants to be well. I've never heard anyone say: 'Oh, I'd really like a bit of a headache today.' I would think they were crazy. No-one gets up in the morning and says: 'Oh, wouldn't it be nice to have a bit of a headache today!'

But some people say: 'God has given me an illness in order to keep me humble.' Then when I say to them: 'Do you want me to pray for you to be even more sick, so that you can become even more humble?' - they answer in fright: 'No, no!'

If you have the attitude *that God wants you to be sick*, you will never have faith that He will heal you. Isn't that true? You have to get it inside your head that God wants you to be well. Amen!

Stop being double-minded. We're not talking about your soul being healthy, but about you yourself being well *in every way*.

Do you believe that God wants you to be well?

It's in the book.

You have to change your way of thinking if you believe God wants you to be sick."

*Pastor Charles preaching in Mexico*

## Is Europe different?

"But some people say: 'Yes, but in Europe we see things a little differently!'

That always makes me smile: Because if you are a Christian, you are not just a European, you are a citizen of heaven. So you shouldn't just think like a European. Think like they think in heaven! *I* think like they think in heaven. Change your way of thinking! It will make a difference in your life.

You have to want to be well. God can't force you. You have to want it yourself. That's why Jesus once said to a man: 'Do you want to get well?' (see: John 5:1-18)

He didn't ask what *God* wanted, but what the man wanted. 'Do *YOU* want to get well?'

God wants you to be well. God wants you to be happy. And that's why Jesus asks: Do *you* want that?"

## Think positively

"At the University of California in Los Angeles they carried out a study not that long ago. The study showed that 75 per cent of illnesses are related to stress and negative thoughts. So it can be proven: It makes a difference what you think. What you think is what you believe.

If you read bad news, it has a negative effect on your whole body. But if you listen to good news - it has a positive effect on your whole body.

Imagine that a completely healthy person walks into a doctor's practice to have a health check done. As the doctor is examining him, he suddenly says: 'Oops, what's that lump you've got there? I think you might have a cancer tumor…'

The doctor didn't say that you had a cancer tumor, but just that he thought you *might* have one. Suddenly you whole body says: You have cancer, you have cancer, you have cancer. The fear paralyzes you. Soon you start reading about cancer, tumors and what symptoms one develops. And soon you even begin to develop symptoms. Have you ever had that experience?

Symptoms are a sign that you might have an illness. But it's possible to have symptoms without having the disease. The doctor didn't say that you had a cancer tumor, but your brain has already gone into *overdrive* –you have begun to overreact. Your thoughts affect your whole body."

## To live in a new way

"I would like to teach you how you can win over sickness. And how you can hold onto your healing. It's like when you buy a new car. It's easy enough to buy a new car, but it's harder to maintain it. It's easy enough to buy new clothes, but it's difficult having to wash them all the time…

In the same way, it's easy to be saved and healed, but it's harder to *live in a new way*; to walk in divine health.

If you are going to succeed, you will have to be aware of some powerful players. And the biggest one is sitting in your mouth!"

## The power in Jesus' words

"Read what it says in Mark 11, about Jesus when he curses a fig tree:

'The next day as they were leaving Bethany, Jesus was hungry. [13]Seeing in the distance a fig tree in leaf, He went to find out if it had any fruit. When He reached it, He found nothing but leaves, because it was not the season for figs. [14]Then He said to the tree, "May no one ever eat fruit from you again." And His disciples heard Him say it.'

When Jesus spoke to the fig tree, the fig tree died.

Reading on in verse 20 we read: 'In the morning, as they went along, they saw the fig tree withered from the roots. [21]Peter remembered and said to Jesus, "Rabbi, look! The fig tree you cursed has withered!"

²²"Have faith in God," Jesus answered. ²³"I tell you the truth, if anyone says to this mountain, 'Go, throw yourself into the sea,' and does not doubt in his heart but believes that what he says will happen, it will be done for him. ²⁴Therefore I tell you, whatever you ask for in prayer, believe that you have received it, and it will be yours. ²⁵And when you stand praying, if you hold anything against anyone, forgive him, so that your Father in heaven may forgive you your sins." '

## Words are the biggest power resource in the world

"The fig tree account shows the power in God's word. When God speaks, things just have to move. God created the whole universe by the power of his word. Words are the biggest power resource in the world. Many people don't know that. But words can shake people, words can create pictures, words can heal people and words can kill people…

In the Bible it says that in the beginning: 'God said…' (Genesis 1:3) and his word began to create something new.

God's power comes to you through the words I speak to you.

God's power is in God's words.

When you believe the good news, the miracle happens."

## The angel's words created Jesus

"In the beginning of John's gospel, the Bible talks about the fact that 'the word became flesh'.

'In the beginning was the Word, and the Word was with God, and the Word was God. ²*He* was with God in the beginning. ³Through Him all things were made; without Him nothing was made that has been made. ⁴In Him was life, and that life was the light of men. ⁵The light shines in the darkness, but the darkness has not understood it.' (John 1:1-5)

This is how Jesus was conceived in Mary's womb. (This is talked about in Luke 1:26-38).

An angel appeared with a word from God: 'Mary, you shall give birth to a child.' That word meant that a child began to be created. It says:

'But the angel said to her, "Do not be afraid, Mary, you have found favor with God. ³¹You will be with child and give birth to a son, and you are to give him the name Jesus."'

Verse 34: '"How will this be," Mary asked the angel, "since I am a virgin?" ³⁵The angel answered, "The Holy Spirit will come upon you, and the power of the Most High will overshadow you. So the Holy One to be born will be called the Son of God."'

While the angel was speaking, a child had in reality begun to form inside Mary.

When God, in the beginning, said: 'Let there be light!', there was light.

In the same way, the word came out of the angel and created a child in Mary.

And Mary asked: 'How will this be?'

And what was the answer? The angel said: 'The Holy Spirit will come upon you, and the power of the Most High will overshadow you.'

## What does it mean?

It means that the Holy Spirit takes the word and makes sure that it happens. Mary wouldn't have been given that child if she hadn't believed it. How do I know that Mary believed it? It says in verse 38: '"I am the Lord's servant," Mary answered. "May it be to me as you have said." Then the angel left her.'

When she said that, she believed. She confessed what she believed."

## Is there a spiritual reality behind sickness?

"Cancer has its own life. You can see a difference between cancer and other diseases under a microscope. Cancer looks different too, for example, HIV. What you see through the microscope is alive. Cancer and AIDS each have their own characteristics. Cancer is alive. It grows.

Using chemotherapy, the doctors try to kill the cancer without killing the person. But chemotherapy affects the patient, it damages the body. If the doctors could remove the cancer cells without hurting the body, it would be an enormous breakthrough.

The reason the cancer cells are alive at all is because they have a spirit. If you remove a person's spirit, they die. Everything that has life has it because there is a spirit behind it.

If you cut a tree off at the roots, it will still look green, but after a couple of days it will whither. Why? Because the trees source of power has disappeared.

Because of Jesus' WORD, life was taken away from the fig tree.

If you remove the cancer's spirit, then the cancer will die. If you remove a person's spirit, then they will die. The Bible says that without spirit the body is dead[1].

But how can we remove the spirit from cancer?

The doctors try to destroy the cancer by, for example, giving you chemotherapy. They try to kill the "enemy invaders" in your body without destroying your body. But what they do is like throwing in a bomb. It destroys a lot of things. But they hope that it will destroy the cancer cells without destroying too much else. Perhaps they can hold the sickness at bay for a while.

But now I'm going to show you how to do it God's way."

## I command the sickness' spirit to disappear

"Every spirit of sickness is subject to God's word. Cancer, AIDS, blindness, deafness, stuntedness, blood diseases… Whatever it might be: If it is a sickness which has life, then it's subject to God's word.

When I order the cancer's spirit of sickness to disappear from the sick person's body in Jesus' name, the cancer cells lose their spirit. They die, just like when you cut off a tree at the roots. The tree might continue to look green for a day or two, but it's dead. And soon its leaves and branches begin to whither. The same thing happens to the cancer.

That's what happened with the fig tree which Jesus cursed. He did it to teach the disciples something about faith and the power in his words. He said: 'whatever you ask for in prayer, believe that you have received it, and it will be yours.'

As soon as Jesus cursed the tree, it died, but Mark tells us that it wasn't until the next morning that they saw the result of his words.

It's the same when we heal cancer or other diseases by driving out a spirit of sickness.

The sickness dies, but it can take time before this is apparent, and there can still be consequences of the disease which have to be restored or rehabilitated."

Notes:
1 E.g.: "The Spirit of God has made me; the breath of the Almighty gives me life." (Job 33:4), "as long as I have life within me, the breath of God in my nostrils", (Job 27:3), "he himself gives all men life and breath and everything else." (Acts 17:25)

*Healing in Zimbabwe 2001. Woman who was involved in an accident where 16 people died and many of her bones were broken, is healed.*

# When healing fails to happen...

**Among the many people whom Charles Ndifon tried to heal at Bornholm, was Charles Marcher, of Østermarie.**


*It looked like* Charles Marcher was healed also and could freely move his head after many years of problems with his cervical vertebra. But unfortunately:

"If I am to be completely honest, then it hasn't improved. I still have pain", says Charles Marcher.

"After the meeting a number of people asked me if I had been healed because they had seen my face in the newspaper. And I had to say that I wasn't – not this time."

## Healed once before

The reason Charles Marcher adds the last few words is because he has already experienced divine healing once.

"Yes, it was in the 1970's, when Ian Andrews was visiting Denmark.

I had just thought to myself, I will go forward if he specifically names my affliction. And immediately afterwards he said that there was someone with severe pain in their back. I had a slipped disc at the time.

I therefore went forward for intercession and he crouched down in front of me and prayed. Afterwards I stood up for the first time in years without having to use my arms. I was so happy I shouted, 'It's true! It's true!'

Afterwards I could take off my jacket without problems and I could lift things.

So I know that God can heal", maintains Charles Marcher.

## Stiff neck

Later Charles Marcher developed problems with his neck and cervical vertebra. He was operated on twice, but still has a lot of pain.

But in the beginning of the 1990's he was at the Lottorp Bible Camp in Sweden. During one of the meetings there was a speaker who suddenly paused, and said:

"Someone is sitting here in this room who has been through two operations. God is going to do a miracle with you, but some time will pass first", Charles recalls.

"Birgit and I looked at each other. How could he know that about me?"

"The speaker also pointed to an area of the room and said that the person he had spoken about was sitting there, and asked them to wave to him. I raised my hand because I knew it was me."

"I therefore had great expectations when I went forward for intercession at Ndifon's meeting.

I thought: 'Is it going to be today?' But it wasn't after all. I was actually in more pain when I sat down", says Charles Marcher.

However, he is still sure in his heart that God will one day heal him, as he has promised.

"Because God doesn't lie", he concludes.

## People who don't get healed after all…

This is the most difficult problem in relation to divine healing. And the hardest chapter to write in this book. The subject is incredibly sensitive, and one can easily be misunderstood.

But even so I'm going to risk my neck, because one can't write about all these fantastic healings without also trying to help the people who don't get healed. And perhaps one could hope that a treatment of the subject might help some of those who have been disappointed to move on.

## Why are some people not healed?

I actually don't think Charles Ndifon understands either, in all cases, *why* it doesn't happen. He has some explanations which cover some of the cases. But not all.

Charles himself fully and firmly believes that when he declares a person to be healed, the person is healed. But he also knows that follow-up is necessary, if many people are not going to lose their healing again. He can't give that follow-up himself, because he has to quickly move on to the next person in the endless queue of sick people who are waiting to receive his prayer every night. He often keeps at it until well after midnight – until all the sick people have been taken care of.

It often turns out when he spends a long time with one person that there are several layers of sickness, and that the person is only properly helped

*Charles Ndifon prays for Charles Marcher in Rønne, January the 20th, 2002. It looked like he had been healed - he could look up and down - but afterwards, his neck problem was still there.*

once he or she has been taught how they themselves can "co-operate with the Holy Spirit" to get out of their sick state.

From my conversations with Charles Ndifon I know that it frustrates him a lot that he can't follow-up the healings. He refers to the local churches, but complains at the same time that most of these don't understand how or have the courage to practice a spiritual power Christianity. They prefer a philosophical Christianity where it is more a question of wise and elegant words.

In a last attempt to help his own "patients", Charles even offers to help those who have been healed who want to establish a new church on the spot!

Because he has no doubt that a correct understanding of the Christian message will create faith and make people healthy, both in body and soul.

## Avoid short circuits
In order to come one step further with the problem, we will now look at

some possible explanations for why a person doesn't get healed – at least initially.

## - Could it have something to do with time?

- Even though not everyone gets healed immediately, the healing might well have begun. 15 years ago I read a book on healing. It was written by T. L. Osborn, and my faith was stimulated so much by reading it that as I waited for a bus in Copenhagen, I closed my eyes and prayed for a very annoying eczema which I had had on my hands since I was a child, to disappear – in Jesus name. When I opened my eyes I still had eczema on my hands, and I was a bit disappointed. So it didn't work after all. But after a couple of months I noticed that the eczema had disappeared. And it has actually never come back in the 15 years that have passed since.

So even if healing doesn't appear to happen immediately, it might well have begun, or might happen later. The great Argentinean evangelist, Luis Palau, had also been in some doubt as to whether God heard his prayers, so he began to write them down in a small book. Beside each item he made a note when he received an answer. It quickly became apparent, he said, that he actually received answers to all his prayers, even though the answer was sometimes 'no' or 'wait'.

## - Is the problem with the sick person themselves?

- One has to be careful about giving the sick person the blame. There can be so many reasons which we don't know as to why people are not healed. The problem, for example, could be with the healer, the surroundings, or be the result of demonic influences. And in some cases it looks as if God holds back – for reasons we don't understand.

But the truth is also that the problem CAN be hidden deep in the mind of the sick person. For example, the healer, Orla Lindskov, relates an incident where he prayed for a very sick man at a hospital in Germany. The man himself wanted prayer, and was a believer, so Orla Lindskov couldn't immediately understand why nothing happened. After he got home again, he prayed that he might understand the problem, and later returned to the man in Germany to talk with him about his life. It turned out that there was a big blockage in the past. Over 30 years earlier, the man had been treated very unjustly by a minister, whom he had been unable to forgive. However, Orla Lindskov managed to help the man to reach a point where he could forgive the minister, even though the minister actually didn't deserve to be forgiven. But the sick man forgave him anyway – because he had been forgiven himself by God. Then Orla prayed for the man again, and after a couple of days he could be discharged from the hospital, completely healed.

From countless cases we know that *bitterness* has made many people sick both mentally and physically. It's not until they can forgive their parents or their spouse, or whoever it might be that has committed an offence against them, that they can get rid of their illness and let the healing happen.

It is thus important to tidy up the past and forgive everyone that might have done something. In order to be able to do that, you have to have experienced God's forgiveness yourself.

## - Is it the healer's fault?

- Charles Ndifon says that if a healing fails to take place, he doesn't reproach the sick person, but goes back to himself to work out what he might have done wrong. The problem can actually be with the healer.

But the healer is often limited by whether the sick person wants to receive healing. Jesus once asked a sick person: 'Do you want to get well?' A strange question – of course he wants to, or…?

Several healers have told me that people's resistance to giving up an illness actually plays a bigger role than most people realise. An illness can give security, attention, care, pity, interest – and many other advantages which we wouldn't otherwise receive.

In such cases it probably doesn't help much to pray for healing.

## Can it be due to sin?

- This is a taboo area. If you say that sickness has something to do with sin, you can quickly arrive at the short-circuit that the sick and handicapped have sinned. People believe this in India, for example, where the teachings of reincarnation reward a good life. And the consequence is that anyone who is suffering is guilty of something in an earlier life. I have traveled in India myself several times and seen these poor people sitting, begging beside the roads. Everyone looks down on them.

And also in many primitive cultures people believe that illness is due to sin. But Jesus says something else. (John 9:3)

But sin can possibly be a *barrier* to healing, so it would therefore be wrong to be completely silent on this subject. But what is sin? Many modern people perceive sin as particular actions in the sexual realm, but this is an unreasonable distortion of what the Bible says sin is. Sex is not sin. Sex CAN be sin – for example if you cheat on your partner, sell yourself to prostitution, produce pornography, rape…

But sin is much more than unfaithfulness. Sin is simply everything which separates us from fellowship with God. Sin is everything unloving. Everything selfish. Everything which we know, deep down, is wrong.

None of us can avoid doing something wrong from time to time. Yes, Luther says we sin every day – a lot. Even so, it's not here that the problem lies, because Jesus has taken the blame. The problem arises when someone doesn't want to get out of the sin. If you don't want to give up doing the wrong thing, it can block God's healing and help, it would seem.

## - Can there be a spiritual explanation?
- In our materialistic Western world we have completely gone away from thinking along these lines, but now Ndifon and others are coming along and saying that there is a spiritual reality behind these mental and physical illnesses. And they prove their claims, so to speak, by, for example, driving out a spirit of sickness just by their words – after which the sick can suddenly see, hear, walk or throw off cancer.

That doesn't mean that the doctors have made a mistake when they observe, for example, that a lump has developed in someone's breast. It has happened, and it's because of cancer, and perhaps in some cases one can even establish that the cancer has arisen due to smoking or something similar. That's something tangible.

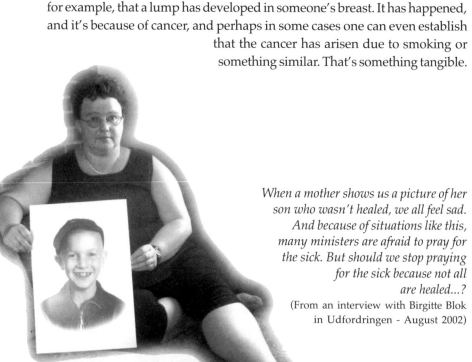

*When a mother shows us a picture of her son who wasn't healed, we all feel sad. And because of situations like this, many ministers are afraid to pray for the sick. But should we stop praying for the sick because not all are healed…?*
(From an interview with Birgitte Blok in Udfordringen - August 2002)

And praise God for the doctors. There is no conflict between what the doctors do and what God does. The doctors make a diagnosis based on what they can measure and see. But Ndifon and others, who believe in divine healing, believe that there is a kind of spiritual superstructure within which one can find the actual cause of the problem.

Within this there exist not just good forces but also destructive ones. And there is a battle taking place between good and evil in the spiritual world.

In some cases people have opened themselves to demonic influence and activity. For example, if someone has sought out occult circles, or exposed themselves to healers who operate on the dark side, evil can have gotten its foot in the door. There are cases where people might experience relief initially, but later become much worse in other areas. What began with occult help against a small physical problem, develops into dependence on the healer, and eventually bigger and bigger inexplicable physical and mental problems arise.

Within the New Age movement there are many positive people who really want to help others. They are seeking, and that's good. After all, Jesus says: "Ask and it will be given to you; seek and you will find; knock and the door will be opened to you." (Matthew 7:7) But unfortunately some get so mixed up in the alternative world, that they come under the yoke of demons.

Ndifon has told me of cases – and others have confirmed similar cases – of such clear demonic activity that the person has lost control of themselves. For example, Ndifon says:

"Some times when we are trying to heal a sick person we run into a resistance we don't understand. Then we ask the person to say, for example, 'Jesus is my Lord'. If the sick person really is possessed, the demon will react. Once there was a deep voice which answered from a woman's body: 'No, she's mine! She's mine!' Then we command the demon to leave. Sometimes the sick person screams or groans or throws up, but then the problem is solved. They are free, they have peace, and they get healed.

Evil cannot stand against the power in Jesus' name.

Paul writes, "Jesus Christ gave Himself for our sins to *rescue us* from the present evil age" (Galatians 1:4). This is not talking about physically removing us from the world, but that we are spiritually removed from *the world of evil*.

Christianity is, after all, all about the fact that Jesus died and rose again to conquer the power of evil. Even though evil still rages in the world, it is now possible to get help, and according to the Bible, at the end, God will break into

*It appears to be easier for the poor people in Africa to receive healing by faith - perhaps because many don't have any other choice than to trust in God.*

*A woman from Zimbabwe has just given up her crutch in these pictures.*

history and finally establish the world of love which was intended – but which evil spoiled.

### - Is it God's fault that I haven't been healed?

- No, as this book clearly indicates, God doesn't wish us any evil. On the contrary. *Evil comes from the evil one.* As we have also discussed, there is a lot of bad theology around about God sending sickness in order to teach us something – or so that we can honor him with our sickness. Ndifon clearly rejects this.

However, for the sake of completeness, we have to also say that there are places in the Bible which can be interpreted as saying that God, in *isolated* cases, permits evil to have a certain power, in order for good to win an even greater victory. (Especially the book of Job and Revelation).

Another aspect is that even though sickness is something evil, out of suffering can come positive effects. We often learn more through suffering than when everything is going well. This is an issue which Ndifon doesn't have much to say about, but which is still part of the total picture.

It is just important that we do away with the incorrect perception that God is behind every kind of accident, or that it is God's will that sickness and accidents happen. No, both sickness and accidents are the result of the ravages of sin and evil in the world. In paradise, there was neither sickness nor any form of suffering. The Bible also says that there won't be any in heaven or on the new earth which God has promised to create when the old one has fallen apart.

God doesn't send illness and suffering. He suffers with us. And he transforms the evil we have to endure into something good.

### - Why doesn't God just intervene?

"But if God is almighty, why doesn't He just intervene?", some object. "Why doesn't He just wipe out evil?"

"No, because then we would also be wiped out", a thoughtful man once answered. God has given people an independent will and the opportunity to choose between good and evil. This is where the whole problem lies. Again and again we choose evil – dressed up as good. The world was transformed from a paradise into a very harsh world. But the good news is that "the one who is in you (Jesus through the Holy Spirit) is greater than the One who is in the world" (1 John 4:4).

Evil has lost the battle, and it loses its power, the more we receive God's power and "God's kingdom".

The New Testament mentions "God's kingdom" 66 times, which Jesus encourages us to do everything possible to enter into. Yes, better to do without an arm or an eye than to miss out on it. But it's hard for a rich man, he says, and unless one becomes like a child, one cannot enter it. It often appears to be heaven – eternal life – that He is talking about. But at the same time, He says in Mark 9:1, "I tell you the truth, some who are standing here will not taste death before they see the kingdom of God come with power." And in Luke 10:9 he says: "Heal the sick who are there and tell them, 'The kingdom of God is near you. '".

It is apparent from the many references that God's kingdom is something which will be fully manifested at some point in time, but which is already partly in operation.

Healings are like a foretaste of God's kingdom. Even though God's kingdom is not in full operation yet – and will only come completely when Jesus returns, "God's children" have authority to make use of its power – if they just have a tiny bit of faith.

*I command you deaf spirit in the name of Jesus: Come out!*

# An attempt to sum up

## - So is it fact or fiction?

After having followed Charles Ndifon at a number of meetings, heard his teaching and seen the results, we have to ask ourselves:
- Is it fact or fiction?
I am personally not in any doubt that it's fact. It's really happening. I have spoken to many more than are mentioned in this book. And everyone who takes part in the meetings can satisfy themselves that miraculous healings are taking place. But it often takes many years before those who have been healed come forward with their personal stories, if they remember to at all!

It's quite common for people to NOT talk about their healings. As a rule it's only the most spectacular healings we hear about. Just think about Henriette from Odense, who was crippled by multiple sclerosis, but was healed in just 5 minutes. Now she can play football and climb trees – and is bubbling with life. But do the doctors believe? No, its taboo!

## The other side of the coin

Unfortunately, not everyone is healed, and not all the healings last. This can be because people don't receive the necessary teaching, but it understandably leads to disappointment and distrust. This represents a big follow-up task for the churches – whether they by teaching and intercession can contribute to a later healing – or just provide caring support.

We hope that this book can also contribute to a better understanding of this - because churches *have been* wanting in this area. People today are like lambs without shepherds in the spiritual world. We are raised to believe that there isn't more to life than what we can see and touch. Now we are discovering that there is after all.

The church has known this all along. But instead of believing it, preaching it and practicing it, it has just adapted to the reigning worldview. Perhaps out of ignorance – or has intellectual and professional arrogance closed some theologians' eyes to "the power of the Spirit"?

## What is the secret?

The next question must be whether Charles Ndifon makes use of special techniques or methods in order to achieve his fantastic results.

If I had imagined beforehand that there might be manipulation or acting involved, then through attending the meetings and digging around behind the scenes, and talking with those healed, I would have been thoroughly convinced that there isn't.

Charles Ndifon is exactly what he claims to be. He doesn't use hidden tricks or hypnosis or any other forms of manipulation. (There are, as is known, other healers, hypnotists, etc., who do, and they can in some cases also achieve certain limited results. But they belong to an entirely different category).

The astonishing truth is that Charles Ndifon is a believer who – in contrast to many of us – has taken Jesus' promises literally and is living them out in their fullness.

That is why he experiences the Spirit's power – the Holy Spirit's power.

I have listened to tapes, seen videos, read articles, heard Charles preach (if you can call it preaching, it happens so informally) and have spoken with him for hours. I had imagined that there must be a special secret since he can perform so many healings – and so easily. But after all this I simply have to conclude that there is no other secret than what we can all read in the New Testament, namely: *Believe in the Lord Jesus, and you will be saved.*[1]

But there are two things which need to be linked to this:

## Salvation is all-encompassing

1. When Charles Ndifon reads the word "salvation", he understands the word in it's full meaning, as it was explained in the chapter entitled: "Salvation = healing".

One can discuss theologically whether this is the correct interpretation. I myself bridled when I heard him interpret salvation in this way. This is because, throughout my Christian education, I have never been given any genuine teaching on healing. Rather the theologians I have heard and whose books I have read have clearly distinguished between the spiritual and physical aspects. Salvation is exclusively understood as being rescued *after* death – from damnation (hell) for eternity together with God (heaven).

Charles Ndifon doesn't reject the idea that salvation involves salvation for eternity – i.e. life after death. He believes that *too,* because in reality his theology is very simple; he believes what Jesus says. And Jesus himself mentions heaven and earth several times as a reality after death.[2]

And the way that Jesus uses the word salvation, it refers in the majority of cases to people who are *healed*, and to whom Jesus declares "Your faith has *saved* you". So Charles Ndifon concludes that *salvation also includes healing*.

## Faith is more than hope

2. The second thing is that Charles Ndifon understands more by the word *faith* than we are used to – both in the worldly and the church contexts. Faith is not just *hope*, but "certain confidence in what you hope", as it is written in the Heb. 11:1. Faith is "being sure of things you don't see". Yes, one could add "being sure of things you don't see YET". Because faith here is about expecting something which will definitely be fulfilled – in one way or another.

Ndifon makes miracles happen because he really believes. I have never met a single person who has such faith as Charles. He is not content just to talk piously about faith – he doesn't talk piously at all! - but he *acts* in faith. For the sake of this faith he risks his name and reputation by challenging the very worst of diseases – cancer – AIDS – yes even missing eyes and legs – and he maintains without compromise that God can and will heal *all*.

## Can faith move mountains - ?

Then there are those that say, "Yes, faith can move mountains". But have you tried it?

People generally forget who it was who said those words. It was Jesus Himself, and He said them to *those who followed Him*. He wasn't just talking about faith in general either, but faith in the fact that *God* would answer.

Jesus gave his followers authorization to use the power in his name. John writes later about this authorization, "[1]Yet to all who received Him, to those who believed in His name, He gave the **right** to become children of God ." (John 1:12). The word translated as "right", is *excusían*, which means power, authority, unrestricted freedom to act. The word is used here to refer to the authority God gives to those who believe. Other translations, for example, the Revised Standard Version, use the word **power**, "But to all who received Him, who believed in His name, He gave **power** to become children of God;"

So Jesus didn't just say generally that "faith can move mountains" – but that: "if *you have faith* as small as a mustard seed, *you can say* to this mountain, 'Move from here to there' and it will move. Nothing will be impossible *for you*." (Matthew 17:14-20)

He is not just talking about psychological forces either. Because although believing in a cause or believing in yourself can give good results, if you believe, for example, in a rock, it won't lead to miracles. At least not the kind of miracles we are talking about here, where people, in a very short period of time, are set free from both their pain and their life threatening illnesses. He is talking about the power of the Spirit.

## Cursed doubt...

The opposite of faith is doubt. And doubt is definitely not God's invention. Doubt creates distance and blockages. Doubt is like the snake in Paradise who says, "Did God really say...?"

Ndifon attempts, time and time again to remove doubt in those who are seeking healing. Doubt is the greatest obstacle to receiving salvation – and all the other blessings from God.

It is also quite obvious that whoever doubts that God exists, will also have trouble believing that the God who perhaps doesn't even exist, can do anything.

And whoever believes that "God exists", but doubts that God is *good*, will have trouble believing that God wants to do anything good for him.

And even those who believe that God is good – as Christians generally do – can often doubt that God really wants *all* people to be *healthy*. In any case, one can easily doubt that God wants to make *me* healthy.

The latter can be because one has been raised with a theology and perception of God where one believes, for example, that God is so exalted that He doesn't care about our small defects. But Jesus says: Pray about *anything*.

## Jesus removes doubt

If we were still in any doubt about *what God is like*, Jesus has swept any doubts aside – because Jesus is the perfect picture of God's being; He is, after all, His son. And He did good from morning to evening and "died for His friends"... Greater love simply cannot be found.

So now we *know* that God wishes us well. Therefore Charles Ndifon doesn't doubt, either, that God wants to save (and heal) all people. Because with salvation comes physical healing and all kinds of other blessings as well.

The reason why God's goodness and healing is not yet found in all people is that there is still a battle going on between good and evil in the world. And unfortunately, according to the Bible, this battle will continue until the day

Jesus comes again to re-establish God's will for the world. John *(in Revelation 21:3-5)* saw it in a magnificent vision and heard a loud voice speak about the future:

*Now the dwelling of God is with men,*
*and He will live with them.*
*They will be His people,*
*and God Himself will be with them and be their God.*
*⁴He will wipe every tear from their eyes.*
*There will be no more death*
*or mourning or crying or pain,*
*for the old order of things has passed away."*
*⁵He who was seated on the throne said, "I am making everything new!"*

Until that happens we still continue to live in the midst of sickness and many other problems. But we can still experiences glimpses of "God's kingdom" in operation here and now, if we believe and don't limit the Holy Spirit's power to work.

## We can close this book by concluding:

1. Healings in Jesus' name are happening today. The examples are too numerous and too convincing for them to be explained away any longer.

2. Healings take place, not only where Ndifon is present, but can happen anywhere where people have childlike faith in Jesus and act in the same way.

3. Healings in Jesus' name are not a modern peculiarity, but a natural part of primordial Christianity which has been lost in modern theology. That is why many of our churches are so spiritually desolate and powerless.

4. Faith is a critical prerequisite for experiencing Christianity's power. Only when you *act* in faith, are the promises fulfilled.

5. A number of people do not get healed. At least not initially. But there is no one single reason for this. And even if someone doesn't immediately experience healing, it can happen after a delay or following later prayer.

6. There is still a lot we can neither understand nor theologize about.

7. God's Spirit continues to be the sovereign, unpredictable factor.

## Don't go into stalemate

There are still a lot of unsolved riddles in relation to healing which are not answered in this book. And which might never be answered.

229

But what I have learned myself through spending so much time with this subject is that one shouldn't go into stalemate. It's easy to be disappointed and it's easy to misunderstand and be offended. But then you miss out on the treasure.

Anyone who wants to can turn what I have written here and use it against me. It's very easy. I am expecting that there will undoubtedly be many offended objections to what I have put forward here. And some people are always content with what other people think.

Unfortunately many of us close the door on healings and other supernatural aspects of Christianity, because we doubt or are afraid of what other people say. And so we put up with a powerless imitation of the fantastic positive message which Jesus and his first followers preached.

That's just too stupid!

But having read this book, you can no longer be in any doubt that there is more to Christianity than what is normally preached. And with Ndifon's teaching and the rest of the book in general, you have hopefully received help to go further and discover the treasure which is waiting for those who seek it.

*For everyone who asks receives; he who seeks finds; and to him who knocks, the door will be opened.*

[9]*"Which of you, if his son asks for bread, will give him a stone?* [10]*Or if he asks for a fish, will give him a snake?* [11]*If you, then, though you are evil, know how to give good gifts to your children, how much more will your Father in heaven give good gifts to those who ask him!*

(Matthew 7:8-11)

Notes:
1 E.g., "Believe in the Lord Jesus, and you will be saved—you and your household" (Acts 16:31-32).
2 "You snakes! You brood of vipers! How will you escape being condemned to hell?" (Matthew 23:33 and Mark 9:43
Also, for example, in Matthew 5:29, 30, 10:28, 23:15, 33, Mark 9:45, 47, Luke 12:5, John 3:16-21.

# Appendix:
# Promises, exhortations and prayers about divine healing

**There are lots of promises in the Bible about healing. Many of these are, of course, said to particular persons at particular times. But Charles Ndifon, and others who believe in divine healing in Jesus' name, believe that since God is the same, we can also believe in these promises today – and be healed.**

## Suggestion for daily meditation

Instead of just reading through all these Bible verses, you could, for example, read one of the verses each morning and meditate on it/think about it or pray and say thank you for the promise throughout the day. If you have a Bible you could consider looking up the verses and seeing them in context. The references in brackets after each verse indicate where they come from in the Bible. The verses below have been taken from the New International Version (NIV) translation of the Bible.

But for you who revere my name, the sun of righteousness will rise with healing in its wings. And you will go out and leap like calves released from the stall. **(Malachi 4:2)**

If my people ... will humble themselves and pray and seek my face and turn from their wicked ways, then will I hear from heaven and will forgive their sin and will heal their land. **(2. Chronicles 7:14)**

"Come, let us return to the LORD. He has torn us to pieces, but He will heal us;

He has injured us, but He will bind up our wounds. **(Hosea 6:1)**

Trust in the LORD with all your heart and lean not on your own understanding; [6] in all your ways acknowledge Him, and He will make your paths straight. [7] Do not be wise in your own eyes; fear the LORD and shun evil. [8] This will bring health to your body and nourishment to your bones. **(Proverbs 3:5-8)**

Do not let them out of your sight, keep them within your heart; [22] for they are life to those who find them and health to a man's whole body. **(Proverbs 4:21-22)**

Above all else, guard your heart, for it is the wellspring of life. 24 Put away perversity from your mouth; keep corrupt talk far from your lips. **(Proverbs 4:23-24)**

The Spirit of the Sovereign LORD is on Me, because the LORD has anointed me to preach good news to the poor. He has sent me to bind up the broken hearted, to proclaim freedom for the captives and release from darkness for the prisoners, **(Isaiah 61:1)**

So if you faithfully obey the commands I am giving you today-to love the LORD your God and to serve Him with all your heart and with all your soul- 14 then I will send rain on your land in its season, both autumn and spring rains, so that you may gather in your grain, new wine and oil. 15 I will provide grass in the fields for your cattle, and you will eat and be satisfied. **(Deuteronomy 11:13-15)**

Be careful, or you will be enticed to turn away and worship other gods and bow down to them. 17 Then the LORD's anger will burn against you, and He will shut the heavens so that it will not rain and the ground will yield no produce, and you will soon perish from the good land the LORD is giving you. **(Deuteronomy 11:16-17)**

Who, then, is the man that fears the LORD? He will instruct him in the way

chosen for him. 13 He will spend his days in prosperity... **(Psalm 25:12-13)**

O LORD, You brought me up from the grave; You spared me from going down into the pit. **(Psalm 30:4)**

Blessed is he who has regard for the weak; the LORD delivers him in times of trouble. 2 The LORD will protect him and preserve his life; ... 3 The LORD will sustain him on his sickbed and restore him from his bed of illness. 4 I said, "O LORD, have mercy on me; heal me, for I have sinned against you." **(Psalm 41:1-4)**

Praise the LORD, O my soul; all my inmost being, praise his holy name. 2 Praise the LORD, O my soul, and forget not all his benefits- 3 *Who forgives all your sins and heals all your diseases,* 4 Who redeems your life from the pit and crowns you with love and compassion, 5 Who satisfies your desires with good things so that your youth is renewed like the eagle's. **(Psalm 103:1-5)**

I will not die but live, and will proclaim what the LORD has done. **(Psalm 118:17)**

But He was pierced for our transgressions, He was crushed for our iniquities; the punishment that brought us peace was upon Him, and by His wounds we are healed. **(Isaiah 53:5)**

Give ear and come to me; hear me, that your soul may live. **(Isaiah 55:3)**

I will guide him and restore comfort to him, 19 creating praise on the lips of the mourners in Israel. Peace, peace, to those far and near," says the LORD. "And I will heal them." **(Isaiah 57:18-19)**

232

Heal me, O LORD, and I will be healed; save me and I will be saved, for you are the one I praise. **(Jeremiah 17:14)**

For I take no pleasure in the death of anyone, declares the Sovereign LORD. Repent and live! **(Ezekiel 18:32)**

I will search for the lost and bring back the strays. I will bind up the injured and strengthen the weak, but the sleek and the strong I will destroy. I will shepherd the flock with justice. **(Ezekiel 34:16)**

After two days He will revive us; on the third day He will restore us, that we may live in His presence. **(Hosea 6:2)**

"See, he is puffed up; his desires are not upright- but the righteous will live by his faith. **(Habakkuk 2:4)**

# Words from the New Testament on healing

Heal the sick, raise the dead, cleanse those who have leprosy, drive out demons. Freely you have received, freely give. **(Matthew 10:8)**

...That is why I did not even consider myself worthy to come to you. But say the word, and my servant will be healed. **(Luke 7:7)**

Heal the sick who are there and tell them, 'The kingdom of God is near you.' **(Luke 10:9)**

On hearing this, Jesus said to them, "It is not the healthy who need a doctor, but the sick. I have not come to call the righteous, but sinners." **(Mark 2:17)**

... It is by the name of Jesus Christ of Nazareth, whom You crucified but whom God raised from the dead, that this man stands before you healed. **(Acts 4:10)**

Is any one of you in trouble? He should pray. Is anyone happy? Let him sing songs of praise. [14]Is any one of you sick? He should call the elders of the church to pray over him and anoint him with oil in the name of the Lord. [15]And the prayer offered in faith will make the sick person well; the Lord will raise him up. If he has sinned, he will be forgiven. [16]Therefore confess your sins to each other and pray for each other so that you may be healed. The prayer of a righteous man is powerful and effective. [17]Elijah was a man just like us. He prayed earnestly that it would not rain, and it did not rain on the land for three and a half years. [18]Again he prayed, and the heavens gave rain, and the earth produced its crops. **(James 5:13-18)**

Dear friend, I pray that you may enjoy good health and that all may go well with you, even as your soul is getting along well. **(3. John 1:2)**

(Jesus says): "I am the living bread that came down from heaven. If anyone eats of this bread, he will live forever. This bread is my flesh, which I will give for the life of the world." **(John 6:51)**

Just as the living Father snt t Me and I live because of the Father, so the one who feeds on Me will live because of me. **(John 6:57)**

"This is the bread that came down from heaven. Your forefathers ate manna and died, but He who feeds on this bread will live forever." **(John 6:58)**

Jesus said to her, "I am the resurrection and the life. He who believes in Me will live, even though he dies; **(John 11:25)**

Before long, the world will not see Me anymore, but you will see Me. Because I live, you also will live. **(John 14:19)**

For to be sure, He was crucified in weakness, yet He lives by God's power. Likewise, we are weak in Him, yet by God's power we will live with Him to serve you. **(2. Corinthians 13:4)**

He himself bore our sins in His body on the tree, so that we might die to sins and live for righteousness; by His wounds you have been healed. **(1. Peter 2:24)**

## Exhortations

There are many exhortations in the Bible about living rightly and doing good. Most of them are addressed to the Jews, but many of them apply generally to everyone who believes in God.

"Honor your father and your mother, as the LORD your God has commanded you, so that you may live long and that it may go well with you in the land the LORD your God is giving you. [17] "You shall not murder. [18] "You shall not commit adultery. [19] "You shall not steal. [20] "You shall not give false testimony against your neighbor. [21] "You shall not covet your neighbor's wife. You shall not set your desire on your neighbor's house or land, his manservant or maidservant, his ox or donkey, or anything that belongs to your neighbor." **(Deuteronomy 5:16-21)**

Walk in all the way that the LORD your God has commanded you, so that you may live and prosper and prolong your days in the land that you will possess. **(Deuteronomy 5:33)**

The LORD your God will circumcise your hearts and the hearts of your descendants, so that you may love him with all your heart and with all your soul, and live. **(Deuteronomy 30:6)**

This day I call heaven and earth as witnesses against you that I have set before you life and death, blessings and curses. Now choose life, so that you and your children may live. **(Deuteronomy 30:19)**

...and that you may love the LORD your God, listen to His voice, and hold fast to Him. For the LORD is your life, and He will give you many years in the land He swore to give to your fathers, Abraham, Isaac and Jacob. **(Deuteronomy 30:20)**

Reckless words pierce like a sword, but the tongue of the wise brings healing. **(Proverbs 12:18)**

A wicked messenger falls into trouble, but a trustworthy envoy brings healing. **(Proverbs 13:17)**

234

"Lay hold of My words with all your heart; keep My commands and you will live. 5 Get wisdom, get understanding; do not forget My words or swerve from them. 6 Do not forsake wisdom, and she will protect you; love her, and she will watch over you. 7 Wisdom is supreme; therefore get wisdom. Though it cost all you have, get understanding. 8 Esteem her, and she will exalt you; embrace her, and she will honor you.
**(Proverbs 4:4-8)**

Leave your simple ways and you will live; walk in the way of understanding.
**(Proverbs 9:6)**

A greedy man brings trouble to his family, but he who hates bribes will live.
**(Proverbs 15:27)**

For I take no pleasure in the death of anyone, declares the Sovereign LORD. Repent and live! **(Ezekiel 18:32)**

"Seek me and live; **(Amos 5:4)**
Seek good, not evil, that you may live. Then the LORD God Almighty will be with you, just as you say He is.
**(Amos 5:14)**

When Jesus saw him lying there and learned that he had been in this condition for a long time, He asked him, *"Do you want* to get well?" **(John 5:6)**

"Make level paths for your feet, so that the lame may not be disabled, but rather healed. **(Hebrew 12:13)**

# Prayers about healing

The book of Psalms in the Old Testament is like a prayer book. David, in many of his psalms, cries out to God for help. Many believe that these psalms (and prayers) have been included in the Bible so that we can turn them into our own. Consider reading the whole psalm in each case.

Be merciful to me, LORD, for I am faint; O LORD, heal me, for my bones are in agony. **(Psalm 6:2)**

I said, "O LORD, have mercy on me; heal me, for I have sinned against You."
**(Psalm 41:4)**

Do good to your servant, and I will live; I will obey Your word.
**(Psalm 119:17)**

Let your compassion come to me that I may live, for Your law is my delight.
**(Psalm 119:77)**

Sustain me according to your promise, and I will live; do not let my hopes be dashed. **(Psalm 119:116)**

Your statutes are forever right; give me understanding that I may live.
**(Psalm 119:144)**

Let me live that I may praise you, and may your laws sustain me. **(Psalm 119:175)**

Pray for the peace of Jerusalem: "May those who love you be secure. **(Psalm 122:6)**

Lord, by such things men live; and my spirit finds life in them too. You restored me to health and let me live. **(Isaiah 38:16)**

Heal me, O LORD, and I will be healed; save me and I will be saved, for You are the one I praise. **(Jeremiah 17:14)**

Blessed is the man who ... delights in the law of the LORD, and on his law he meditates day and night. ³He is like a tree planted by streams of water... **(Psalm 1:1-3)**

## Pitfalls –

Good advice from the Bible on how one can avoid getting involved with evil spirits.

**Test the spirits – to see whether they are from God**

Dear friends, do not believe every spirit, but test the spirits to see whether they are from God, because many false prophets have gone out into the world. ²This is how you can recognize the Spirit of God: Every spirit that acknowledges that Jesus Christ has come in the flesh is from God, ³but every spirit that does not acknowledge Jesus is not from God. This is the spirit of the antichrist, which you have heard is coming and even now is already in the world.

⁴You, dear children, are from God and have overcome them, because the one who is in you is greater than the one who is in the world. ⁵They are from the world and therefore speak from the viewpoint of the world, and the world listens to them. ⁶We are from God, and whoever knows God listens to us; but whoever is not from God does not listen to us. This is how we recognize the Spirit of truth and the spirit of falsehood. **(1 John 4:1-6)**

**The evil spirit will return, if you are spiritually empty**

When an evil spirit comes out of a man, it goes through arid places seeking rest and does not find it. ⁴⁴Then it says, 'I will return to the house I left.' When it arrives, it finds the house unoccupied, swept clean and put in order. ⁴⁵Then it goes and takes with it seven other spirits more wicked than itself, and they go in and live there. And the final condition of that man is worse than the first. That is how it will be with this wicked generation." **(Matthew 12:43-45)**

**You have to know what you're dealing with**

Some Jews who went around driving out evil spirits tried to invoke the name of the Lord Jesus over those who were demon-possessed. They would say, "In the name of Jesus, whom Paul preaches, I command you to come out." ¹⁴Seven sons of Sceva, a Jewish chief priest, were doing this. ¹⁵One day the evil spirit answered them, "Jesus I know, and I know about Paul, but who are you?" ¹⁶Then the man who had the evil spirit jumped on them and overpowered them all. He gave them such a beating that they ran out of the house naked and bleeding. **(Acts 19:13-16)**

### It's not enough to simply believe God exists

You believe that there is one God. Good! Even the demons believe that—and shudder. **(James 2:19)**

### Knowing Jesus as Lord

Therefore God exalted Him to the highest place and gave Him the name that is above every name, [10]that at the name of Jesus every knee should bow, in heaven and on earth and under the earth, desolate [11]and every tongue confess that Jesus Christ is Lord, to the glory of God the Father. **(Philippians 2:9-11)**

### Confessing Jesus as Lord, saves

That if you confess with your mouth, "Jesus is Lord," and believe in your heart that God raised him from the dead, you will be saved. **(Romans 10:9)**

### To deny Jesus is to deny God

No one who denies the Son has the Father; whoever acknowledges the Son has the Father also. **(1 John 2:23)**

### Spirits which don't come from God

This is how you can recognize the Spirit of God: Every spirit that acknowledges that Jesus Christ has come in the flesh is from God, [3]but every spirit that does not acknowledge Jesus is not from God. **(1 John 4:2-3)**

### Be careful not to add anything

Watch out that you do not lose what you have worked for, but that you may be rewarded fully. [9]Anyone who runs ahead and does not continue in the teaching of Christ does not have God; whoever continues in the teaching has both the Father and the Son. [10]If anyone comes to you and does not bring this teaching, do not take him into your house or welcome him. [11]Anyone who welcomes him shares in his wicked work. **(2 John 1:8-11)**

### Consistency between word and spirit

Now about spiritual gifts, brothers, I do not want you to be ignorant. [2]You know that when you were pagans, somehow or other you were influenced and led astray to mute idols. [3]Therefore I tell you that no one who is speaking by the Spirit of God says, "Jesus be cursed," and no one can say, "Jesus is Lord," except by the Holy Spirit. [4]There are different kinds of gifts, but the same Spirit. [5]There are different kinds of service, but the same Lord. [6]There are different kinds of working, but the same God works all of them in all men. **(1 Corinthians 12:1-6)**

### Not enough to be religious

"Not everyone who says to me, 'Lord, Lord,' will enter the kingdom of heaven, but only he who does the will of my Father who is in heaven. [22]Many will say to me on that day, 'Lord, Lord, did we not prophesy in your name, and in your name drive out demons and perform many miracles?' [23]Then I will tell them plainly, 'I never knew you. Away from me, you evildoers! **(Jesus in Matthew 7:21-23)**

# The Apostle's Creed

I believe in God, the Father almighty,
creator of heaven and earth.

I believe in Jesus Christ,
God's only Son, our Lord,
who was conceived by the Holy Spirit,
born of the Virgin Mary,
suffered under Pontius Pilate,
was crucified, died, and was buried;
he descended to the dead.
On the third day He rose again;
he ascended into heaven,
he is seated at the right hand of the Father,
and He will come again to judge
the living and the dead.

I believe in the Holy Spirit,
the holy catholic church,
the communion of saints,
the forgiveness of sins,
the resurrection of the body,
and the life everlasting.

**The author**

HENRI NISSEN trained at the Danish School of Journalism. He was formerly a public relations officer at the Danish Federal Parliament, and he transformed the monthly Christian magazine, Udfordringen (The Challenge) into a weekly newspaper in 1985. He has traveled in and written about Asia, America and Africa, and recently worked at an African radio station in Cameroon for three years. He is now employed part-time as a communication consultant for the Lutheran World Federation in French-speaking Africa. He has written several books that have been translated into other languages. His next book project is about the remains of Noah's Ark on the border between Iran and Turkey. The book is expected to be released in 2003.

238